THE CHURCH MOUSE

The Church Mouse

Leadership Lessons from the Magic Kingdom

CHRISTOPHER W. PERRY

THE PILGRIM PRESS

CLEVELAND

★ **DEDICATION** ★

I would like to dedicate this book to my wife, Renae, who has spent many years sharing and enhancing my love for Disney, and to my boys, Caleb and Cole, who make Disney magical every time I get to experience it through their eyes.

The Pilgrim Press, 700 Prospect Avenue, Cleveland, Ohio 44115
thepilgrimpress.com
©2011 by Christopher W. Perry

Scripture quotations, unless otherwise noted, are from the New Revised Standard Version of the Bible, ©1989 by the Division of Christian Education of the National Council of Churches of Christ in the United States of America, and are used by permission. Changes have been made for inclusivity.

SUSTAINABLE FORESTRY INITIATIVE | Certified Fiber Sourcing
Label applies to the text stock | www.sfiprogram.org

Printed in the United States of America on acid-free paper

15   14   13   12   11   5   4   3   2   1

Library of Congress Cataloging-in-Publication Data

Perry, Christopher W., 1974–
    The church mouse : leadership lessons from the Magic Kingdom /
    Christopher W. Perry.
        p. cm.
    Includes bibliographical references.
    ISBN 978-0-8298-1874-1 (alk. paper)
    1. Christian leadership.   2. Walt Disney Company—Management.   I. Title.
BV652.1.P44 2011
254--dc22   2010048078

CONTENTS

★

★ FOREWORD ★

D r. Christopher Perry has captured the right idea for the Christian church to ponder: Become relevant or start a slow decline towards irrelevancy. At Walt Disney World, we continually find ways to stay relevant as our guests and Cast Members evolve in their thinking, what they want, and how they want it from one generation to the next.

The world is a vast, quickly changing landscape. The rate of change is faster than ever and will continue to speed up as the world becomes more interconnected and people more dependent upon each other. Being relevant is no longer an option for any organization, religious or otherwise. It is a matter of survival. *The Church Mouse: Leadership Lessons from the Magic Kingdom* does a wonderful job of presenting the case for major change in the church. Christians need and want spiritual support and advice, but they want to receive it in a way that is uplifting and educational and in a way that makes sense to them. Don't simply recycle lessons and stories from two thousand years ago without showing the application for today. At the same time, don't only focus on the past. Tell current stories about how to live a good life and how to deal with the challenges we are all facing in our relationships with each other and with God.

The Church Mouse is an excellent textbook and manual on how churches can start to become places where people of every age wake up in the morning and want to go. This movement will require a new mindset, new energy, new sermons, new ways to attract and engage members, and a completely new environment and culture that is exciting and relevant, focused on today's challenges.

Kids of all ages jump up and down when they know they are going to Disney World. The church needs to create this same excitement. Read this book. No, study this book and start to figure out how to do in your local church what we do at Disney. It is not magic that makes Disney World work. It is the way we work that makes it magical.

LEE COCKERELL
executive vice president (retired),
Walt Disney World Resort

featured speaker on the Executive
Speaker Series at the Disney Institute

author of *Creating Magic: 10 Common
Sense Leadership Strategies from a Life
at Disney*

★ ACKNOWLEDGMENTS ★

This book wouldn't have been possible without the help of a lot of folks:

First, thanks to my wife, Renae, who made sure my ideas made sense and my writing style didn't wander too far off. Also, thanks to Dad, Dr. Wayne Perry, for being such a great sounding board for the ideas found within this book.

I need to thank the people of Robinson Springs United Methodist Church for putting up with my Disney fanaticism, for serving as such a great laboratory for these ideas, and for their patience in allowing me the time to write.

Thanks to my dear brother in Christ, Dr. Bryan Sims, for his wisdom and insight as we discussed the ideas found within this book.

Thanks to all of my fellow Disney fanatics from Intercot.com who gave me the needed feedback to help refine these ideas: Lisa Hiteshew, Christine Hammerschlag, Mikki Young, Heather Stevenson, and Rita Shicunoff.

Thanks to all of the Disney Cast Members who took time to share their insights and love of Disney with me, especially Jennifer and Kevin Brassard, Alice Bass, and Phil Card.

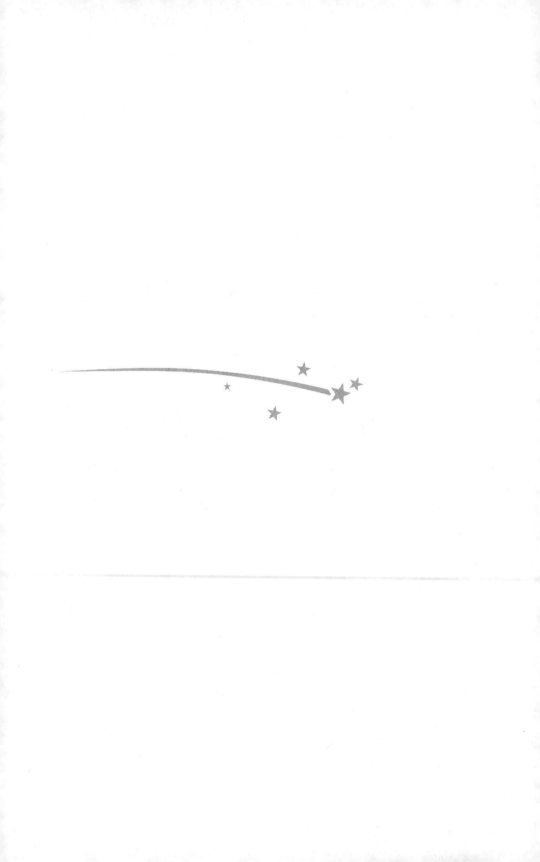

INTRODUCTION ★ THE DISNEY DNA

I only hope that we don't lose sight of one thing—
that it was all started by a mouse.

—WALT DISNEY

Hello. My name is Chris and I'm a Disneyaholic. (Everyone say, "Hi, Chris.") I realize that's a fairly big revelation since we just met, but it is important that you know where I stand. My family and I love all things Disney. We try to go to the parks at least every other year. We adore the movies. My boys prefer watching Playhouse Disney (renamed Disney Jr. in 2011) cartoons in the morning over anything else. Several rooms in our house are themed in Disney. My wife, Renae, and I went to Walt Disney World for our honeymoon and even had a Mickey and Minnie Mouse cake topper at our wedding. Is it excessive? Probably. But at least you understand my opening confession.

Now that you have had a glimpse into my mania, I want to state that all of the preceding has very little to do with my desire to write this book. These things are only the surface of my true fascination with Disney. As I visited the parks and watched the movies I began to wonder why millions of people, including my family, were willing to spend so much of their hard earned money year after year to go to a theme park. I enjoy going to Six Flags over Georgia with my family for a day, but we would never spend a week there nor would we be willing to pay the same level of pricing. What is the difference? Both have well-established characters. Both have high thrill rides, such as roller coasters, and more tame rides aimed at a wider audience. Both have shows. The difference is what inspired the book you now hold and what we will discuss over the next few pages.

For years I have taken notes on my observations in the Walt Disney parks. I have spoken with many "Cast Members" (Disney's term for employees). I have read countless books on Disney principles. While there are plenty of books on applying Disney principles in the corporate world, I have not seen one that applies those principles to the area of Christian leadership. I think church leaders can learn a lot from Disney. This book is not aimed at pastors, but all church leaders—elders, deacons, committee chairpersons, church school teachers, and every other type of leader in the church. All can benefit from the lessons Disney has to teach. While we in the church are not out to put on a show, we are very interested in attracting and retaining "guests" (the Disney term for customers). We both seek to create an experience for those who visit us. We both seek to convey a message as creatively as possible.

Disney's job is to accomplish their goals so that their guests are entertained. If the guests go away happy then they will return to spend more money and the company's bottom line will grow. In the church we are out to bring people into an encounter with the Living God. The Holy Spirit reaches out to people through us, but the church is the voice, hands, and feet of God encountering those who need to hear from God. Our aims go way beyond profit margins. Should we not, then, put at least as much effort into achieving our goals as Disney does towards achieving theirs?

A WHOLE NEW WORLD

Before we delve into the specifics of Disney leadership, I would like to take a moment to examine the culture that makes these principles particularly poignant for the church today. I do not think anyone would disagree when I say that the world is a much different place than it was twenty years ago. For many churches that fact alone is a source of great tension as well as frustration for its leaders. We are firmly in the postmodern age, which is, as Disney's Aladdin sings, "a whole new world."[1] The problem I, and many within the church, have had with the postmodern movement is that it is incredibly difficult to define. Even the term "postmodern" tells us more about what it is not (modern) than what it is.

The "modern" age began with the Enlightenment and was based in rational thought, scientific method, and sound thinking. Technology was seen as the savior of humanity and religion began to be dismissed as a crutch for the weak. These ideas are clearly seen in the science fiction writings of the 1950s where the future world was seen as a utopia driven by science and technology.

During the nineteenth and twentieth centuries the church saw many apologists rise up to show the world why Christianity was rational. Their arguments were firmly entrenched in logic and fact. The goal was to convince the mind in order to reach the heart. Atheism was seen as the primary enemy of Christianity.

Somewhere along the line things changed. Atheism is no longer the enemy. It is rare to find an atheist in today's world. Our global culture is extremely spiritual. I have jokingly told my congregation that people today will worship a mailbox if you give them half a chance. Religions of every shape are extremely popular, with the singular exception of Christianity. While all other world religions are experiencing growth, Christianity continues to decline in Europe and North America.[2] Our enemy now is the danger of irrelevance. The church is in danger of becoming a relic of a bygone era, not because of its message, but because of its practices.

Scholars have debated as to when, exactly, modernity started to crumble. Some say it was the hippies of the 1960s that started the change. Others claim the 1986 explosion of the Challenger space shuttle shattered the faith in technology. This book does not exist to debate when it started, but I do think we need to recognize the change that has happened. In 2000 Leonard Sweet wrote a book about the postmodern movement in which he described the new culture as seeking something EPIC—experiential, participatory, image-driven, and connected.[3] It is this idea that Disney does so well and that the church must learn if we are to reach a new generation with the gospel—the good news of Jesus Christ.

Scripture clearly teaches us that Jesus is "the same yesterday and today and forever."[4] We know that the message of the gospel never changes. Our methods, though, must evolve if we are to be relevant to the culture around us. This can be particularly difficult in established churches where the first response to any new idea is the fatal motto: "We've never done it that way before." It is up to you, as a leader within your church, to walk your frightened, and sometimes very stubborn, congregation through this process. It is a process that pastors cannot accomplish alone. Only with the help of dedicated, wise lay leadership, working together with the pastor, can the church navigate these rough waters and find relevance in the community.

Walt Disney had embraced Sweet's EPIC idea long before Sweet or anyone else thought of it. When Disneyland opened on July 17, 1955, it presented something no one had ever seen before. The idea of amusement park rides had been around for years, but Disney immersed every ride within a story, so that it ceased being just a ride and turned into an experience.

Let me give you an example of how "experiential" looks by comparing two similar roller coasters. Six Flags over Georgia has a roller coaster called the Ninja. It's painted red and black and has a vaguely Japanese-styled entrance. Beyond that, there's nothing "ninja-ish" about the coaster. Certainly I do not feel as if I have experienced the ninja culture when I finish. It's a metal coaster that goes upside down, does a couple of corkscrews and is a fairly fun ride. Compare that to a ride at Disney's Hollywood Studios in Walt Disney World called Rock 'n' Roller Coaster. Here you approach a building designed like a recording studio, inside and out. As you enter you find records on the walls and decorations related to Aerosmith, the band featured on the ride. Before actually getting on to the ride you are led into an area that looks very much like a live recording studio, where you view a preliminary show featuring Aerosmith. The preshow is vital to the experience, as it gives you the story behind the ride: Aerosmith has to get to their concert but you, their fan, have been given a backstage pass and a limo ride to the concert. You then exit into the ride loading area, which is perfectly themed to look like a back ally. The roller coaster cars are designed to look like a stretch limo. The "limo" moves into position and you hear a rock-concert style countdown from ten. Upon reaching zero the limo is launched from zero to sixty miles per hour in slightly less than two seconds using a slingshot-type technology similar to what is used by the U.S. Navy to launch airplanes off of carriers. At this point you are off on a wild ride with Aerosmith music playing and a theme all around you that looks like the Los Angeles freeway at rush hour. The exit dock looks like the backstage area at a coliseum. By the time the ride ends you have been immersed in this idea of going to an Aerosmith concert, and you walk into an area with Aerosmith playing a live concert on a big screen. Rock 'n' Roller Coaster is not a ride. It's an experience from start to finish. The concept—a metal roller coaster with a couple of loops and corkscrews—is identical to that of Six Flags' Ninja. The execution is an entirely different matter. Both are acceptable as forms of entertainment, but one leaves a much longer lasting impression than the other.

Within the church we face a similar issue. Most of our worship services, regardless of style or denomination, contain the same elements: sermon, singing of some kind, prayer, offering, communion (Lord's Supper, Eucharist, or whatever you call it in your tradition), baptism, and maybe special music or drama. The execution of those elements is what will determine whether your congregation has an experience they will remember or if they go through the motions and forget most of what happened by Monday morning. Any style of worship can create an experience and involve people in the story, but it takes a lot of effort and energy.

Continuing with Sweet's acronym, Disney also excels at the concept of being participatory. While on a recent trip to Disney World I saw a very simple, but powerful, example of this in the Magic Kingdom. Disney does many things to involve its guests in the various shows and parades, but tucked away in a quiet corner near Cinderella's Castle is Fairytale Gardens, where there are multiple daily shows of Storytime with Belle. The magic begins as soon as you enter the Fairytale Gardens, which has crumbling walls and looks centuries old. The story of the location is that it is a part of ancient ruins from the 1300s near Cinderella's Castle and is now being restored. Belle comes out with two helpers and spends about fifteen minutes telling her story as seen in *Beauty and the Beast*.[5] Through the course of her story, Belle picks children from the audience to come onstage and play the various characters. She also brings up one adult man to play the part of Beast. The participants are given very simple costumes and, anytime the characters are supposed to speak, Belle tells them exactly what to say. There are no pyrotechnics, music, or "wow" factor, yet I saw children and adults alike enthralled. The children (and man) called up on stage had huge grins on their faces as they walked out of the theater. I also heard children who were not picked asking their parents to come back so that they could be picked next time.

Another example is the Jedi Training Academy at Disney's Holly-wood Studios. My oldest son, Caleb (now nine years old), was picked to participate in this show, and he recalls it as one of his best memories of all time. Like Storytime with Belle, the concept is simple. In the initial version of the show, the Jedi Master would use the Force to find several young "padawans" in the gathered crowd who were strong enough in the Force for training. Guests with children would return show after show in hopes of being picked. As of 2010, the method was altered so that children now stand in line to participate instead of the Jedi Master randomly choosing them out of the crowd. The previous system meant that a child might attend ten shows in a day and never be picked. Obviously, in such a case, both the child and parents would walk away frustrated and disap-pointed, something Disney never wants to see happen. While the change may have taken away some of the "magic" of the selection process, at least now all the children know they will have a chance to participate if they are willing to wait in line. Wouldn't it be a great problem for the church to have so many people trying to get into worship that we completely change our system?

As the kids are brought onstage they are given simple brown robes and $10 "flick-out" plastic light sabers that you can buy at any Walmart. Each child is then "trained" in the Force and given a chance to battle Darth Vader one on one when he appears. Children will stand in line an hour or more to be able to participate in the show. When was the last time your church offered something so simple and yet that people were clamoring to experience?

Both of these examples demonstrate that you do not have to invest large amounts of money to get people excited. Beyond the initial outlay of set and costumes, both of these experiences are minimal in cost for Dis-ney, yet they remain wildly popular. Why? Because everyone loves to participate, to become part of the story, as opposed to sitting back and watching. We remember best that in which we are personally involved. Too often a church service is a show (and a poor one at that) where there is no participation from the congregation at all. True worship means participation. The word "liturgy" comes from the Greek word *leitourgia* which means "the work of the people." Not "the work of one guy standing up front while everyone else watches." In the truest original sense of the word it meant people working together in an act of public service. The *leitourgia* was something done together for the good of the state or city. To bring it into the modern application, liturgy (regardless of your worship style, every service has a liturgy) should mean all Christians, laity and clergy, working together to perform a public act of devotion and love to God.

If you want your congregation, adults and children alike, to be excited about worship, then find ways for them to participate. Challenge (and assist) the pastor to go beyond "fill-in-the-blank" style worship planning each week and find creative ways to involve the congregation in the greatest story ever told. It would be very easy for a church to tell its scripture for the day in the exact same way Belle did. The outlay for a few costumes would be minimal, but the impact could be eternal.

Let's continue on the EPIC journey with "image-driven." Image is the primary means of communication in today's culture. Image is not just a picture. Effective use of image creates an entirely new experience and unleashes a range of emotions that words alone cannot. For instance, Disney brings the monorail around Epcot instead of directly into the train station in order to fix the image of what the guest is about to experience firmly in their minds. It heightens excitement and anticipation. As these expectations are fulfilled, the next time a guest experiences the same images his or her excitement becomes even greater.

The proverb "a picture is worth a thousand words" has been around a long time, but in previous cultures the spoken or written word has been primary. This is no longer the case. Here we find perhaps the most difficult transition for church leaders. For hundreds of years preaching has been viewed as a verbal art. Seminaries spend countless hours teaching future preachers how to carefully craft their words, how to adjust their inflection, and how to speak clearly and effectively. While that model is not completely useless by any means, it is no longer the primary means through which we will impact the lives of those in worship. However, because this has been the primary model for so long, it has become ingrained in the mindset of almost everyone in the church. Churchgoers, especially those raised in the church, expect the proclamation of the gospel to be one person standing up front giving a prepared statement. But because the postmodern culture is so image driven, they often miss the message when it is presented in strictly a verbal manner.

For thousands of years traditions of various cultures were passed down orally, from one generation to the next. Each culture worked endlessly to ensure that the cultural knowledge was never lost. Around 4,000 BCE, the Sumerians began carving their stories into clay tablets. While this made transmission of thoughts portable, it wasn't a very practical system due to the weight of the clay tablets. Then, around 3,000 BCE, the Egyptians invented papyrus. Finally, thoughts could be written onto a medium that was lightweight and fairly durable. The invention of papyrus created a radical paradigm shift in the ancient world. While many traditions were still passed on orally, slowly the world began transitioning to the written word for the preservation of ideas and history. While the spoken word remained the primary means of communication, the written word made it possible for ideas to be passed along to new generations. Today we are seeing a similar paradigm shift as the world moves from the spoken word to the image as the primary means of communicating ideas.

Disney understands this paradigm shift. Pay attention to how carefully they craft their commercials—both in print and video. I attended a Creative Ministry conference at Walt Disney World put on by Leadership Nexus. One of the presenters was Jeff Larson, vice-president of marketing for Disney parks. He walked us through the entire process of crafting these images for Disney marketing, step by step. Every image, font, and layout they use is carefully thought out to achieve a desired emotional reaction—usually that of you immediately jumping on your computer and booking your next Disney vacation. They go through tons of revisions to make sure they get it just right. Like other companies, Disney could just throw some words and a logo together and say "good enough," but they understand the power of the image to say more than words. One of the best examples was the "Joy to the Small World" ad they ran in December 2009.[6] Throughout this commercial, children from all over the world are shown boarding Peter Pan's pirate boat filled with pixie dust and arriving in the midst of the magic of Walt Disney World at Christmas. The emotional impact, on parents especially, is incredible. Yet, outside of the lyrics of "It's a Small World," no words were used. Not even a "come to Walt Disney World" tag at the end.

The church too often misses the power of image. I've seen pastors who think they are postmodern because they put white text on a blue background in PowerPoint and put it on a screen. This is approaching the situation from the modern concept of the word as the primary means of communication. Image is not just what is on the screen, but what is all around us as we worship. Image can be on the screen, yes, but it can also be on the altar, in the foyer, or in the children's area. Image is anything visual that helps bring home the impact of the message for the day. Jesus certainly understood the power of image. How often did he say, "The kingdom of heaven is like . . ."? Jesus never spoke just in words. He painted pictures. He pointed out metaphors. He helped connect the nebulous and difficult to understand truths of theology with the finite human brain by looking at the world around him and using familiar images. Images are what provide the "a-ha!" and serve as a constant reminder of the message every time we see that image in the future.

Many lay leaders might be reading this section and thinking, "I hope the pastor is reading this." However, it's not just the pastor's job. In order to create a worship experience like I'm talking about, everyone has to pitch in. When I led two different styles of contemporary worship at First United Methodist Church in Huntsville, Alabama, I had a planning team that helped with every aspect. My job, as pastor, was to give my team the "big picture." I told them what my scripture was and the main idea of the sermon. Then I would exegete the passage for them so that they understood the context and history of the passage. The team and I would then brainstorm together until we decided on the most effective image to convey the "big idea." After that it was mostly out of my hands. We had a music team, media team, drama team, and environmental team who all got to work making the worship experience image-driven. While this model was used in a contemporary worship setting in that situation, it can work regardless of the style of worship. Good lay leaders don't wait on the pastor to do everything. They join together with their pastor to create a team that helps bring the message of the day to life.

The final piece of the EPIC pie is "connected." We live in a world that is more wired than ever and yet more disconnected than ever. Through voice mail, cell phones, texting, social networking, and other means, I can instantly reach anyone, yet feel completely isolated at the same time. I might have five hundred "friends" on Facebook, yet no one I can call upon when I need help.

Disney has tried to tap into this desire for connection through several media. They had the "virtual Magic Kingdom" online for a few years and still have other online games. They heavily promote the Disney Vacation Club as a way to connect with other Disney fans. They have recently been promoting the "Mickey Mom's Panel" as a way for Disney fans to connect and share ideas. Their big connection, though, is family. Over and over they emphasize in their ads that their parks are about families, especially multiple generations, being together. That idea is very appealing in households where dual-career parents are desperate to find time with their kids.

This is one area where the church is primed to excel, yet we rarely do. A study of the book of Acts quickly reveals that the church is meant to be all about community—sharing all of our lives with each other (see, for example, Acts 2:42–47). That is what the postmodern community desperately wants. It is what the local church should be able to provide above all else. This is one area where church size and resources don't matter.

My youngest son's favorite shirt comes from Disney's Hollywood Studios. Written on the front is "Judge me by my size, do you?" and on the back is Yoda, wearing Mickey ears and holding a Mickey ice cream bar, looking up at a sign reading, "you must be this tall to ride this ride." I think a lot of churches feel similarly. We look around and think, "You must have this resource or this amount of money or this many people before you can minister to your community." I hear from my own folks sometimes that they don't feel like they've been a Christian long enough, or haven't memorized the Bible enough, to effectively minister. I have news for you: You can be a Christian for three seconds and welcome someone. You can have a budget of $0 and make people feel loved.

Robinson Springs UMC, where I currently serve, is not overrun with resources. We do not have a large budget, a fancy children's area, or a worship center that will wow anyone (except with its history). But the laity of the church "get" that they can be the most welcoming church around, and, the idea of "family" is part of the DNA in our church. They help every person who comes through the doors to feel connected. Pastors can't force that and certainly can't pull it off on their own. It's up to the lay leaders of the church to make this effort. How?

The key is to be intentional in forming that community. Communities rarely form by accident. This is where Disney's principles of intentionally building a culture, which we will discuss in the next chapter, come into play.

Sweet's EPIC definition of postmodern culture is by no means the final word on the subject. We could define postmodernity many different ways, but I feel the EPIC acronym provides a succinct way to understand how the culture has shifted, how Disney has met that shift, and how the church can learn from those principles. Someone once said, "Insanity is doing the same thing over and over again but expecting different results."[7] If the church continues to act as if the modern world still existed then the world around us will dismiss us as irrelevant. This is truly a "whole new world." It is time for the church to wake up and engage that world with the best tools we can find.

While your church may not have Disney's budget or resources, many of the principles that Walt built into the Disney Corporation will apply directly to making you a more effective leader. The ideas that Disney builds into the DNA of all of its Cast Members will serve to make you and your fellow church members more effective servants of Christ. Disney does not do everything perfect. No corporation does. But we can learn a lot from them. I hope you enjoy the journey and that what you learn in these pages will be used by God to bring people in your sphere of influence into a closer relationship with the Divine.

★

LIVING INTO THE LESSON

1. How does your church see the world's culture? Are you Church versus Culture, Church Working with Culture, Church Transforming Culture, or Church Ignoring Culture?

2. How do you think the world around you views your church? Have you asked any nonchurch members about their perception of your church?

3. How does your church try to relate to our changing world? Where do you excel at reaching the culture? What can you as a church do better?

4. Why is the concept of an experience versus a ride important? Share a time when an "experience" of worship impacted you. What details made it better than any previous service?

5. How do you think being part of the show changes your experience?

6. How is your church worship participatory? How can you invite more participation?

7. Jesus constantly used images to connect the people with his message. How effective is your church in using imagery, both in and outside of worship?

8. What do you need to do in order to experience genuine community? How do you evaluate your current effectiveness in creating community?

ONE ★ CREATE YOUR CULTURE

It's kind of fun to do the impossible.

—WALT DISNEY

During a scene in one of my favorite movies, *The Hunt for Red October*, a young CIA analyst, Jack Ryan, is trying to convince a U.S. Navy admiral that the captain of a rogue Russian submarine is trying to defect, not attack the United States. The admiral is skeptical of Ryan's assertions and asks, "What's his plan?" Ryan is confused and the admiral states, "Russians don't [go to the bathroom], son, without a plan."[1]

This statement perfectly sums up the mindset of the Disney Corporation. Part of the reason that Disney has been so highly successful is that they are intentional about creating the environment in which their people work. All of the chapters of this book will deal with an aspect of this culture. None of these ideas were created by accident. From the ground up Disney is intentional about hiring the kind of people who will fit their culture, training them how to interact within that culture, then deploying them to further that culture. Walt Disney's personal definition of leadership sums up this idea: "The ability to establish and manage a creative climate in

1

which individuals and teams are self-motivated to the successful achievement of long-term goals in an environment of mutual respect and trust."[2]

Careful examination of Walt's words reveals the secret of creating your culture. "Establish" and "manage" are words that scream "intentionality." A lot of planning, prayer, and courage are required to intentionally create a culture that will accomplish great things for God. Many churches tend to think of the pastor as the one who creates the culture of the church. While a pastor can guide the culture, he or she—unless the founding pastor—rarely creates it. Even then the pastor doesn't really "create" it. The culture of every church is really a mish-mash of all the individual narratives ("life stories") brought by the members. The founding pastor can create a theme around which all the individual narratives organize themselves, but those individual narratives are still a part of the culture. In other words, the people of your local church are not programmed robots. It is possible to establish an overarching story (the "metanarrative") that everyone participates in, but the individual parts are not eliminated. When you are leading cultural change you are not brainwashing people, not trying to have them eliminate their personal story in favor of the church's, but giving them a bigger story onto which they can join their individual story.

Pastors come and go, but it is the lay leaders who stay year after year (or generation after generation in the case of my church) who truly drive the culture of the church. Most often this is done unintentionally. The culture just "happens." If we look at Disney we'll see that they have made sure culture does not just happen. The difference is me blindly reaching into a refrigerator, throwing whatever I pull out into a blender, and hoping something edible comes out versus creating a meal by using specific ingredients at the right time.

Walt also spoke of the specific environment he wanted in his company, which is one where the employees are "self-motivated" in an environment of "mutual respect and trust." Those are very specific goals. Do you think those things can happen by accident? Walt knew exactly what kind of environment he wanted within his company and he took the appropriate, intentional, steps to make it happen. Pat Williams calls Walt a "futurist" and says, "Futurists don't just predict the future. They make the future happen."[3] The environment Walt envisioned when he and his brother, Roy, founded the Disney Brothers Cartoon Studio in 1923 (re-named Walt Disney Productions in 1929) is still alive and well within the Disney Corporation today because they made it happen. While dwelling on Walt's words we must ask: If Disney can succeed in this manner, why does the church seem to struggle so with its culture?

CULTURAL BARRIERS

All church leaders are generally presented with one of two issues. First, we inherit a culture. The church I currently pastor, Robinson Springs United Methodist Church (henceforth usually referred to as RSUMC), was founded in 1828. When I arrived in 2006 there was definitely a culture already in place. I love the history of this church. The founding pastor, Peyton Bibb, was the brother of the first two governors of Alabama. Our current sanctuary, built in 1845, still has the original floor, pews, pulpit, and communion railing. The original bell still hangs in the tower and the children love to ring it after church every Sunday. The slave balcony still exists much as it did in the pre–Civil War days in which it was built. The church has an entire room just to showcase its history, including a hammer used to build the church, the original communion set, and the original pastor's Bible.

I love standing in the pulpit each week and thinking about how many times God's Word has been preached from that very spot. I love to pray at the communion railing and think how many lives have been changed kneeling around this very rail. While all of this history is a wonderful thing, it comes with a price. I inherited a church with 178 years of baggage. That's not a completely bad thing. The people of this church have 178 years of faithfulness as a foundation for their service. They have a rich history of which to be proud. The problem is that any changes that need to be made take a long time because the culture of the church is already so ingrained. As Bob Iger, CEO of the Disney Corporation, said of Disney's own well-established culture, "The baggage of tradition can slow you down. I'm not going to eliminate that," he added, "but I'd like to reduce it significantly."[4]

This is the issue that so many church leaders encounter. Some of you may have been in your current church since you were in the womb. You know the history inside and out. Others of you may be fairly new to your congregation, but no matter when you joined I'm sure it hasn't taken you too long to discover your church already has a well-developed culture.

While the length of time the church has been in existence factors into the equation, it is not the sole determining factor in cultural change. Whether the church is 182 years old, as mine now is, or whether it's two years old, a culture still exists. I spent two years planting a church and discovered that within a few months a definite personality had emerged within the church. I have spoken with countless church planters who were shocked to hear "that's not how we do things" from their six-month-old congregation. As Stacey Snider, CEO of Dreamworks, commented about Iger's desire to implement some changes as Disney, "This is a legacy business and whenever someone challenges that legacy, you have pushback."[5] I'm sure many of you reading that statement will offer a hearty "amen!"

The church is a "legacy business." We've been guarding the legacy of Christ and all the faithful Christians who have gone before us for two thousand years. We've been the guardians of God's story much longer than that. Any time you try to change something people are going to have strong emotional reactions. Disney faces these issues every time they change or remove a ride at one of their parks. Two of my favorite rides as a kid in Epcot were Horizons and World of Motion. I was horrified when Disney removed them and went through an actual grieving process the next time I visited the parks after the rides were closed. Those emotional attachments to the memories from our childhood cause us to react strongly when they are challenged or changed.

Within the church this reaction can be even stronger. To many in the older generations it will feel as if their experience of church is being invalidated when things are changed. They grew up cherishing the rituals and traditions of worship as they knew it. They were taught that to do these certain things brought honor and glory to God. Now they are being told those same things are "irrelevant" and a hindrance to bringing new people into the church. The things that they view most fondly are, in essence, being declared as "not good enough." Is it any wonder why some churches are torn apart when they try to add a new ministry or worship style?

If you are going to be successful in leading within your church, you must become an anthropologist in order to successfully navigate these cultural landmines. You are in a foreign culture with its own language, rituals, personality, and cultural landmines. You might have been in the church for twenty years, but if you weren't born in that church, as I often hear in small town Alabama, "you ain't from around here." Many leaders within the church have become frustrated when an idea they had for a new ministry was derailed because they violated part of the existing culture of the church. I often see new Christians, full of energy and ideas, blindsided by the culture of their new church family. Even experienced leaders who are well-respected and have been in the church for years encounter conflict within their church when they have one vision of how the church should be and the current culture of the church is completely different. A common frustration I hear is from church leaders returning from a conference with fresh vision and ideas, and then not being able to understand why they meet so much resistance in the implementation of those ideas. In the end, the leaders often become disillusioned and frustrated and return to the "status quo."

So what should you do when you feel passionate about a vision from God and the church culture does not fit that vision? What usually happens is you either become resigned and defeated, allowing yourself to be swept along by the status quo, or you directly challenge the current culture of the church, which creates conflict. When this scenario involves a pastor, that conflict often leads to the pastor leaving or church members checking out, both physically and/or mentally. When this situation involves laity I often see these once promising lay leaders fade into the background so that they can blend in or they fall away entirely, ending up in another church, if anywhere at all. Neither solution is healthy. The key, as we will learn from Disney, is to implement intentional, incremental cultural change.

Many of you might look at Disney and assume that such a creative, well-resourced company could never identify with the cultural challenges of bringing change within a church, but in a comment about Winston Churchill, one of his heroes, Mr. Iger said, "Churchill balanced heritage and innovation. There are big lessons in that for Disney. Our brand is so powerful because of our heritage. But you've got to innovate, and not just in terms of what is new today but what will be new far into the future."6 These words should be memorized by every church leader—combining heritage and innovation is what the church is all about. We cannot forget the two thousand years' worth of heritage every church has inherited, nor even the two to 182 (or more) years of heritage found within the local church. To dismiss the foundation we've been given would be to throw away everything that has been sacrificed so that we could meet as the church today. However, if we dwell on that heritage, and never advance past it, then we will never accomplish anything great for God. God will always do something great, but dwelling on the past might result in us missing what God wants to do in the present. This is especially true of lay leaders, as opposed to clergy, as laity usually invest many more years in one particular church than does their pastor.

The laity usually do a good job of guarding their heritage, but they also need to protect the future by not treating the past like an idol. This does not mean you need to follow every new idea the pastor, or any person, throws out to you. Part of being good stewards of what God has given us is to, as Proverbs 4:5 instructs, seek wisdom and good judgment in everything we do. I tell my congregation constantly to not buy into everything I say simply because I'm the pastor. I'm human and, therefore, am susceptible to being wrong. Often. I rely on my lay leaders to bring their wisdom and good judgment to the table so that together we can figure out what God wants for us.

The second issue that church leaders often encounter is flying by the seat of their pants. This is especially common in a new church situation or in an existing church where rapid growth occurs. Any time you have a large influx of new people the status quo will change. The question becomes, who dictates where that change will lead? The honest answer is, usually, the crowd.

When I was in college at Mississippi State University I was fortunate enough to participate with the Famous Maroon Band in the Peach Bowl in Atlanta, Georgia. Our game was to be played on New Year's Day, so several of us went to watch the "big peach" drop for New Year's Eve in downtown Atlanta. Once the countdown to midnight was complete and everyone was through celebrating I knew where I wanted to go. My objective was to get to the MARTA station so that I could catch a train back to my hotel. The crowd had other ideas. There were so many people packed into that small space that I literally could do nothing other than be swept along by the crowd. I desperately tried to fight my way across to the train station, but I eventually had no choice but to go along with the crowd or risk being trampled.

This illustration demonstrates how many leaders feel when confronted by the crowds of their congregation. You might have a vision for a new ministry in your church, but the momentum of the crowd is so over-whelming that you begin to feel that there is no choice other than to ride out the wave. You are swept along feeling like you have no say in the di-rection of your church, which is a frustrating place to be.

Once the crowd has momentum there is little that can be done, ini-tially, to change its course. When I was in downtown Atlanta I should have looked around, seen the impending problem, and intentionally sta-tioned myself in a position to reach my objective while avoiding the stam-pede. Because I got caught up in the moment I was whisked away before I knew what was happening. Every effective leader needs to intentionally position him- or herself to reach the objective without getting caught up in the crowd. If you get caught up in the moment, it's too late.

CHURCH ON MISSION

Having read through the last few paragraphs you may be thinking, "Thanks, Chris, for pointing out the obvious. I already know what the problem is. How do I change it?" I'm glad you asked. And this is where Disney will begin to help us find our way to being more successful for the kingdom, or realm, of God.

Both problems previously noted had the same root cause—lack of in-tentionality. In the case of an existing culture the leadership, both clergy and laity, are forced, through negative feedback and/or positive reinforce-ment, to maintain the status quo. With no plan in place to change the status quo, it will never change. Homeostasis is a property of all living systems—including churches and corporations. In the second scenario the leadership team is flying by the seat of their pants, simply trying to keep up with the rate of growth and change. There's no time to plan.

What if the Titanic had encountered that iceberg on a clear after-noon? What if the captain had paid attention to the warnings and reduced speed? Do you think in either scenario the ship might have avoided ca-tastrophe? The problem was not that the Titanic could not turn. The problem was the speed of the ship combined with the suddenness of the iceberg's appearance made the disaster unavoidable at that point. With different circumstances, a different course, or a different speed the chances are good you never would have known the name "Titanic." So it is with the church. Many of the disasters we encounter in ministry appear so sud-denly that by the time we realize what is about to happen it is too late to do anything about it. This is where intentional planning comes in.

Disney does not open the gates to its theme parks each morning and hope for the best. Every Cast Member has a mission to fulfill and has been intentionally and thoroughly trained in how to fulfill that mission. The mission, whether we are talking about a street sweeper, someone per-forming in a show, a cashier at a restaurant, or an executive working be-hind the scenes, is exactly the same: to make each guest's visit as magical as possible. Each Cast Member plays a different role in making that hap-pen, but the mission unites them all.

This is an important concept for the church. Too often I see churches totally dependent upon, and driven by, the personality of the pastor. All ministry goes through the pastor. This is not the way God intended for the church to function. Paul speaks often about the many gifts found within the church and exhorts each person to use his or her gifts (see 1 Cor. 12 and Eph. 4). No one person has every gift, meaning no one pas-tor, no matter how talented she or he may be, can accomplish all of the ministry. That's where the laity must step up. If all the people do their part, using the gifts God has given them, then ministry is very effective. When everyone sits around waiting on the pastor, then ministry is limited.

The church can use Disney's model of everyone having a function and being equipped to carry out that function in accomplishing the overall mis-sion. What is the mission of the church? Jesus makes it pretty clear that the mission of every local church is to make disciples (Matt. 28:16–20). This involves bringing people to Christ (evangelism), nurturing them in their relationship with Christ (discipleship) and deploying them to minister for Christ (ministry). All Christians have that same mission, but all of us have different roles in accomplishing that mission. At the Disney parks, all Cast Members have the same mission of giving the guests a magical experience. Some keep everything clean, some sell food or merchandise, some perform, some assist with the rides, but all parts perform their functions to the best of their abilities to accomplish the same mission.

High Altitude Leadership is a fascinating book that uses mountaineering as a metaphor for leadership. The authors state that they noticed a real difference in their teams before and after a summit attempt. Before and during the attempt to climb the mountain the team is energized, focused, and working well together. Once the climb concludes they noticed the team begins to fall apart, even with a successful summit attempt. Bickering ensues and they all start putting themselves above the team. It would be normal to assume that a team that had just succeeded in summiting one of the highest mountains in the world would be ecstatic and celebratory. Why did they fall apart? The answer, the authors found, was that the mission was accomplished.[7]

If we are brutally honest then we must admit that human beings are, essentially, selfish creatures, including those within the church. In secular circles we might hear terms like "not a team player" or "selfish" tossed around. But we with a Christian worldview know this as the sin nature. In Romans 3:23 Paul says we're all guilty of falling short of God's standard. Later, in Romans 7, we hear Paul lamenting that, under his own human strength, he is incapable of doing the good that he wants to do. I hear pastors often telling war stories at gatherings and conferences about congregation members with "good intentions" who are running amok. They seem at a loss as to how to bring their wayward sheep back into the fold. One pastor told me, "I feel more like a firefighter than a pastor. Every time I put one fire out another springs up. I'm so busy running from fire to fire that I never get any ministry done." In much the same way, I often have lay leaders from my congregation sitting in my office venting their frustrations about not being able to accomplish the ministry they want because they can't get their team to work together.

How do we overcome this issue of the sin nature? Yes, I realize if we're very holy we can use the good "Christianese" and say, "Only by the power of the Holy Spirit." While that is true, the phrase is more often than not used as a cop-out to not do the hard work. Warner and Schmincke discovered the way to overcome it in mountaineering was by keeping everyone focused on a common mission. Hear me clearly—having a mission statement and being on mission is not necessarily the same thing. It's possible to have a mission statement and never accomplish anything for God. A mission statement is not enough. The mission must be connected to a story that causes us to want to be a part of something bigger than ourselves—that causes us to sacrifice self for the good of the cause.

Mission statements and vision statements became all the rage during the 1990s. Every corporation, and every church, had to have a mission statement. Companies and committees spent hundreds of hours crafting these eloquent statements. Then they were promptly forgotten. Some churches print their mission statement on their website, or bring it up occasionally at charge conference meetings, but if I asked the average person sitting in the pew, rarely can they tell me what the mission of the church is. Even those who can parrot the statement have no real-life connection to it. That is where the church has failed so miserably. We may have a wonderful, eloquent mission statement, yet we've never attached it to a story to make it real—to make people want to give their lives to achieve it.

The mission statement of the Disney Corporation is: "The mission of The Walt Disney Company is to be one of the world's leading producers and providers of entertainment and information."[8] I'm not sure if I asked any of the more than sixty thousand Cast Members who work at the Walt Disney World Resort to repeat that mission statement verbatim that many of them would be able to. A few of them would, but probably the majority would know it more in a summary version. It's not that they haven't heard it or do not agree with it. It's just that mission statements, without a story attached, are boring and useless, no matter how eloquent the language. The genius of Disney is that they know how to create a great story.

One of the most famous examples is that of "Bump the Lamp." I have heard this story told by numerous Cast Members who have been with Disney over the years. If you watch the 1988 film *Who Framed Roger Rabbit*, you can view a scene where Eddie (a live human) takes Roger (an animated rabbit) to the back of the bar to cut off the handcuffs that Roger slapped on them as a joke. In all of the craziness the lamp hanging from the ceiling is bumped and begins to swing wildly. The shadows in the room exactly match the swinging motion of the lamp. That required a lot of extra time and animation to perfectly synchronize. In the end, very few viewers noticed or appreciated what they had seen, but that scene became a mantra for Disney.

Michael Eisner, CEO of Disney from 1984 to 2005, used "Bump the Lamp" as a rallying cry for Cast Members. Every Cast Member goes through Disney's training program, called Traditions. During this program Eisner explained the "Bump the Lamp" concept to the Cast Members and encouraged them to give the extra effort, even when not noticed by the guests, to make the Disney brand the best that it could be. "Bump the Lamp" put a story with the mission statement. Cast Members from all divisions grasped the concept and used it as motivation to go the extra mile, even when they weren't rewarded for the effort. Through this intentional use of the mission statement Disney created a culture of employees (Cast Members) who went beyond only what was expected. No corporation, or church, will gain that effort without intentionality.

Another example of attaching a story to the mission comes from *Beauty and the Beast*. When that movie came out in 1991 everyone remembered the famous catch-phrase sung by Lumiere and the rest of the kitchen: "Be our guest." Disney still uses that phrase today to teach Cast Members how visitors to the parks should be treated—as guests, not customers. A guest is someone to be welcomed in, to be treated with all of the hospitality you can muster. A customer is a buyer, someone you want to purchase something so that you can increase your profit margin. A guest is a friend to be respected. A customer is a "thing" to be used. The two viewpoints are light-years apart and result in a very different attitude toward those who come to your place of business. Do you view those who come into your church as guests to be welcomed with intentional hospitality or do you view them as "customers" who will, hopefully, increase the church's bottom line?

Both the "Bump the Lamp" and "Be our guest" concepts were used by Disney to craft a DNA of hard work and welcoming attitude. Today, when people visit the Disney theme parks they expect something far superior to any other theme park. They expect to not just ride a few rides but to be treated like honored visitors. In general, people do not go to any other theme park with this expectation. Why do they at Disney? Because Disney intentionally crafted that culture.

In the church we have the "greatest story ever told." We have two millenia worth of faithful men and women who have given everything for the cause of Christ. God is doing incredible things in our midst today. It is not for lack of stories that our people are not on mission. It's lack of intentionality. If you are struggling in your church with people bickering and wanting to do their own thing, chances are they are not connected to a mission of any kind. Don't wait for the pastor to create this culture; it is up to all of the leaders to work together to make it happen.

Step one in creating the culture, changing the DNA, of your church is to discover your church's mission and connect people to that story bigger than themselves. By this, I mean find the particular story of when your church is at its best and then connect that to the larger Christian narrative. This mission cannot be just what the pastor wants to do. It has to be something that all of you will rally behind and give your all to supporting. For instance, at RSUMC I saw a church that had an old building and very few resources. We weren't going to have the biggest, best youth or children's programs around. We weren't going to have the best praise band and, certainly, not the best preacher. I struggled to find our connecting point. Through prayer and a lot of discussion with the leadership it hit me: we would be the friendliest, most welcoming church around. We grabbed on to Disney's "be our guest" idea and ran with it. Now the greeting time during worship can last five minutes or more. We have monthly potlucks, weekly fellowship meals, and extra fun events. We refer to the church as our "family." I intentionally have preached, taught, and encouraged every member to welcome every person he or she sees, no matter whether that person is familiar or not and no matter what the person looks like. Now visitors can hardly get five feet inside the door without ten people wanting to welcome them. That shift costs no money—only intentionality. When people visit our church, over and over, we hear how welcomed they felt. This is irrespective of whether or not they choose to make this their church home. The church bought in because hospitality was something near to their hearts. "Be our guest" made sense. That idea connects with the dominant southern narrative of "southern hospitality," which is already ingrained in almost anyone who grew up in the Deep South. Good stories will connect beyond themselves, usually unconsciously. The folks of my church only needed a little intentional pushing in that direction.

A key part of making this effort successful was me working hand in hand with my lay leaders. I did not dictate to them what we would do, nor did they sit back and passively wait on me to tell them. So if you're reading this and thinking, "I need to give this to my pastor so he or she will know what to do," then you've got the wrong idea. Start making these changes in your sphere of influence. This can be in your church school class, in your leadership meetings, or just among friends. Sit down with the pastor and talk about these ideas so that you can all be on the same page. Whatever you do, don't do "nothing." Sitting around wishing for a mission won't make it happen any more than setting up an admiration society for your mission statement will make it change your church.

Mission statements are great, but they are useless unless they are connected to a story that makes them come alive. Don't waste time crafting something eloquent without figuring out how to make it more than words on a page. What are the images and stories of your culture and community that will make your mission come alive? Find those stories, connect your people to them, and watch your mission and ministry effectiveness soar.

The best way to find these stories is by asking the older members of your congregation and community. Find the ones who really know the history and DNA of your church and surrounding community and get their input. By asking their opinions you'll usually gain their buy-in instead of opposition. Plus, you might find some insight and wisdom along the way. Combine their response with those of newer folks—both in the community and the church—to see what a fresh set of eyes and ears can teach you.

Disney did not succeed by simply deciding they wanted to. Once they had their mission connected to a story, the next issue became conveying that story to all the Cast Members. How do you make sure that all members of your team, whether we're talking a couple of hundred like in the local church or tens of thousands as with Disney, have this DNA ingrained in them? It partially comes down to training, which we'll cover in detail in chapter 5, but a large part of the ability to connect people to the story came from having a leader who is an excellent communicator.

An excellent communicator does not necessarily have to be an excellent speaker, and I'm not specifically speaking about the pastor here, either. Being an excellent communicator means that the leader is able to convey ideas and concepts in such a manner that the recipients understand them and incorporate them into their own lives. I have heard many entertaining and charismatic speakers who had little to no impact on my life once their speech was over. If their purpose was purely to entertain, like a stand-up comedian, that is fine. If, however, the speaker is seeking to implement change and I merely walk away entertained, then the speaker was a good speaker but not a good communicator. On the flip side, I have heard speakers who bored me to tears during the presentation, but as I reflected on their words real change came into my life. The ideal situation, obviously, is to have someone both charismatic and a good communicator, but one does not necessarily mean the other.

A good communicator is required in every area of the church. Certainly the pastor has the largest audience on Sunday mornings and, thus, a wonderful opportunity to communicate the vision. But you and every other leader within the church communicate by how you interact with others, how you lead your team, and by the way you speak (or don't speak) about the vision and mission of the church. Church school teachers, small group leaders, and leadership team leaders are often more important than the pastor in communicating the vision because they are the "boots on the ground." When I stand up in the pulpit and communicate the vision, there is little opportunity for dialog. When you gather with fellow believers in a leadership team meeting, however, you can discuss, get input, and clarify among your team so that the vision and mission are clearly understood. Do not assume that mission communication is only the job of the pastor.

SAFETY

I want to take a moment to talk about one specific area of intentionality that needs to be addressed within your church: safety. Over the last year many people were shocked by two accidents that occurred at the Walt Disney

World resort. In July 2009, a pilot of the monorail system was killed due to a safety malfunction. In April 2010, a nine-year-old boy was killed when his bicycle ran off the sidewalk and he hit a Disney bus. Both of these incidents made national news and sent shockwaves through Disney fan site Internet message boards. Why? I live just outside the city of Montgomery, Alabama. There are people killed in accidents on a weekly basis, yet I doubt many, if any, of those accidents are reported even as close as Birmingham, just ninety miles up I-65. So, while these two incidents are tragedies, why would we hear about them? Every other traffic accident that happens in the Orlando area is not broadcast on CNN. Why this one?

The answer is because Disney has intentionally created a culture of safety. Walt Disney World bills itself as "the most magical place on earth" and "the place where dreams come true." People don't die in accidents in "magical places." Accidents have to do with reality, and we're trying to get away from reality when we're on vacation. Here is true reality: between Cast Members and guests, Walt Disney World can have over a hundred thousand people on their property at any given time. That's larger than many cities! What's astounding is not that they have had accidents, but that there aren't more of them. Having driven around the resort property while on vacation, I can also testify to the fact that many folks seem to forget a lot of their safe driving habits when they leave for their vacation, making the low accident rate all the more impressive.

Disney's incredible safety rate, like everything else within their climate, is not an "accident." As we'll talk about later in chapter 4 ("Attention to Detail"), Disney goes out of their way to make sure they provide the most magical environment possible. They want absolutely nothing to ruin the experience for their guests. They monitor all areas of the resort, keep their roads well-maintained, and have security on standby at a moment's notice. I personally experienced this while walking around Epcot one afternoon. I ventured into the restroom at the United Kingdom pavilion and encountered a man doing something highly inappropriate at one of the urinals. I did an immediate about-face and mentioned this to a Cast Member I met right outside the door. He disappeared quickly and in less than a minute a couple of Disney security officers had arrived and escorted this man to a backstage area where, I assume, they removed him from the property. I was amazed at the swiftness of the response and it really helped me feel safer with my children at the park.

I realize that Disney is a public place and they can't keep out all undesirable behaviors. My encounter demonstrates this. Walt Disney World also had a couple of issues with female guests being harassed at the water parks in 2009. In both situations Disney responded as quickly and appropriately as they did in the encounter I witnessed. Reality is that they will never stop all of the "bad guys" from getting in, but they have a plan in place and respond immediately when anything does happen.

This aura of safety Disney creates is why people are so upset when a tragedy does occur, even though with so many people in one location the odds are stacked against a "perfect" safety record. Bad things are just not supposed to happen at a Disney park. This emotional expectation is even more profound within the church. Out in "the world" people understand that bad things happen. Whether the idea is realistic or not, the general public has the notion that nothing bad happens at church.

Most churches refer to the room in which public worship is conducted as the "sanctuary." Merriam-Webster's online dictionary defines a "sanctuary" as "a consecrated place" and "the room in which general worship services are held." There is, however, also a secondary definition for sanctuary: "a place of refuge and protection."[9] We're very familiar with the first definition, but we often don't give as much thought to the second one. The concept, however, goes back, in our faith tradition, to the old Deuteronomic Code establishing sanctuary cities (see, for example, Num. 35 and Deut. 19). There was also a practice popular in many countries well into the nineteenth century whereby a person could go into the church to escape prosecution and/or imprisonment. People see the church as a "safe" place, a place to seek refuge from the evils of the world, and this concept has been ingrained through the centuries.

The difference between Disney and the church is that most churches I know, especially the smaller ones, are not nearly so intentional about making their congregation a "safe" place. Safety is merely an illusion because no thought is given to ensuring that safety. There seems to be an assumption that "nothing bad could happen here." The problem is that one day we'll find out that assumption is wrong to our great cost. The child sexual abuse scandal that has rocked the Catholic Church over the last few years is a perfect example. The crimes committed by these men would be bad in any setting, but, in the public's perception, the fact that these crimes were committed by priests in the church magnifies the severity of the crime.

Let's do a quick quiz to see how safe your church really is. Do you have specifically written requirements for someone to be eligible to work with children? Do you define appropriate behavior between adults and youth group members? Do you have a check-in/out procedure within your nursery? Do you make sure children are never alone with only one adult for any period of time? Do you have a policy about closed doors? If you said no to any of these questions (and I could ask many more) then you have a safety problem within your church.

Large churches have tended to catch on to this issue faster than the smaller ones. Our small churches tend to be more "family" churches where everyone knows everyone and the assumption is that nothing could ever go wrong. Policies to protect your children need to be in place no matter the size of the church. And this is not a job for the pastor or the church council (or whoever the policy making body of your local church is). Every person within the church is responsible for creating a safe environment. But that won't happen unless you intentionally build a culture of safety. Until then the assumption will always be "it's someone else's responsibility."

The United Methodist Church, like some other denominations, has started a "Safe Sanctuaries" initiative to help churches become more intentional about being a safe place.[10] No matter what your denominational affiliation, it is vital that you help your local church to intentionally create a culture of safety. As I've already stated, people let their guard down when they come into the church building. Unfortunately, the predators know this and see the church as a primary target.

Creating a culture of safety takes intentionality, but it does not take a large budget. Procedures such as requiring a criminal background check for all youth and children workers can uncover problems before they start and will discourage predators from coming to your church. Why should they take the risk with you when they can go to a church with no procedures in place? That is a sad, but true, reality. Background checks can generally be done for $8–10, which is relatively inexpensive considering the benefit. If your church budget is stretched thin, it's not wrong to ask the volunteers to pay for their background checks. In fact, that would serve as another means of filtering out those who are not committed to the best interests of those they are seeking to serve.

Other policies to have in place should include sexual abuse reporting, how to handle a stalking type situation (unfortunately common in the church, especially ones with singles programs), age restrictions on watching children, minimum number of chaperones and age requirements for youth trips, policies forbidding an opposite sex chaperone from being with a teenager, have a sign-in and a sign-out policy for the nursery, just to name a few.

This may sound morbid, but part of being intentional is to think of everything that could possibly go wrong and then have a contingency plan in place to respond to it if it happens and prevent it if possible. This really is a job for the lay leaders of the church. Your pastor needs to focus on the pastoral care, preaching, and teaching ministries of the church. I am, essentially, making the same argument here as the apostles did for involving the laity in Acts 6. God calls all of us to different ministries and we're doing a disservice to the church when we expect the pastor to handle it all. This kind of detailed work is best hammered out by committees. Involve people who are directly impacted—parents, youth, nursery workers, and so on. They will give a good perspective on the types of things to protect against and create a much better end product than if everyone looks to the pastor to take care of it all.

Up until now, I've focused almost entirely upon physical safety. If you want, however, to have a successful church, you also need to create an environment of spiritual and emotional safety. If your church is like most, when the "greeting" time occurs, whether before or during worship, the conversation usually goes something like this: (two smiling people approach each other) "How are you?" "I'm fine, how are you?" "I'm fine!" "Good to see you!" "You, too." And they move on to the next person. Does that sound familiar to you? The reality is that one or both of those people may be dying on the inside.

We wear masks to church because we don't feel emotionally safe. I realize there are appropriate things to share in public versus private, but when was the last time someone said to you, "I'm really hurting today. Can we talk after worship?" I hear that sometimes as the pastor, but what I really want to see is the church family ministering to its own members. That will only happen if we feel emotionally and spiritually safe. You don't want someone pouring out his or her every thought and feeling in front everyone on Sunday morning, but we need to break down this idea that you have to be "perfect" on Sunday mornings.

One of the reasons people enjoy the Disney parks so much is that they feel emotionally safe, as well as physically. If you don't believe me, just look at some of the things people wear on vacation. They are definitely not trying to put a front on for anyone. They feel safe to relax and not worry about trying to impress anyone. I'm not saying people should feel free to dress in worship like they do on vacation, but the issue is: Are people trying to impress others during worship or do they feel safe enough to be themselves?

Another example is to look at how people act at the Disney parks. It's not just for kids. Every time I'm at the parks, I see numerous couples on their honeymoons or celebrating their twenty-fifth wedding anniversary without the kids. Even when they are alone as a couple they don't act like "adults" at Disney World. Plenty of grown people will rush to get in line to meet Mickey and the other characters. They will wear the silly hats, scream themselves hoarse during the parades and shows, and laugh until they hurt on the rides. Emotionally, they allow themselves to become kids. And Disney encourages this idea.

Real ministry happens when people feel safe enough to be vulnerable; to share what's really going on in their lives. Because I have intentionally tried to build a culture of safety at RSUMC, I can't tell you the number of times people have said during Bible study, "I've never felt comfortable asking this question in church before, but . . ." and they'll say whatever is on their minds. This safety is not because of the pastor's brilliance. I wish I could take credit, but I really can't. It's because people have learned through relationship building that they can be themselves at this church without fear of rejection.

Building this kind of environment takes two things: time and intentionality. You're not going to have people suddenly sharing their lives overnight, especially if that concept is foreign to your church culture. Secondly, you have to be intentional about building relationships. People often feel safe sharing with the pastor because of the office. I have people call me all the time whom I have never met, but because of my position as a clergy member they automatically spill everything. That's fine for strangers, but within the church it's up to the lay people to build those types of relationships.

I would encourage you to look at starting small group ministries in your church, if they don't already exist. Small groups foster relationships and create an emotionally safe environment that can never be found in a public gathering. Don't think of small groups in a strictly brick and mortar since, either. While face-to-face meetings are ideal, social networking sites, chat rooms, and blogs are other ways to express ideas and communicate. Technology should never replace face-to-face meetings, but if technology can enhance the sense of community among your team and church family, then, by all means, use it.

Another step you can take is to build relationships throughout the congregation. As a church leader, take the time to get to know people. Don't rely only on the pastor to meet the emotional needs of those around you. Model this behavior by being transparent. Allow people to see who you really are, and not just a mask on Sunday morning.

Another aspect to this is to protect those who are vulnerable. For instance, if you hear gossip, put a stop to it. Pastors rarely hear gossip. People know the rules. They know they aren't "supposed" to gossip so they'll usually keep quiet and smile around the pastor, but if you hear it, stop it. Any time gossip exists in the church, no one will feel emotionally safe. After all, if we, together, gossip about Mrs. Jones today, what's to stop your co-gossiper from doing the same with someone else about you tomorrow?

If you can help those around you to feel safe emotionally and spiritually, then you will begin to see lives changed. As people open up about their struggles, God can come in and provide healing. You aren't the one who heals. Nor is the pastor. That's God's area, only. You can be a vehicle towards healing, though, by fostering genuine relationships that allow people to share their lives with you and those around them.

Thinking of safety, both physical and emotional, is ministry at its maximum. Jesus commands us to care for the least and the last, the "vulnerable" populations. By ensuring that every person who walks through your doors feels safe, and actually is as safe as possible, you will open the door to greater ministry.

CONCLUSION

In order to effectively create the climate you, as the leader, envision you must be able to clearly communicate what that climate is. We go back to Walt Disney's definition of leadership where he uses the terms "self-motivated," "mutual respect," "teams and individuals," and "long-term goals." All of those aspects are very clear. Those were the things Walt felt were important to "establish and maintain" the "creative climate" that he was after and that Disney is known for still today. If you cannot clearly and effectively communicate to your people the climate you want to exist within the church, then it'll never happen. No great thing happens by accident. When we are intentional with prayer and planning, then the DNA of the church will move toward the environment you envision.

★

LIVING INTO THE LESSON

1. What is the overarching story or culture in your church? How do you personally engage and further that story?

2. How does meeting the future as it comes differ from intentionally creating the future?

3. How does tradition slow down your church? How does it slow you down personally? Where does tradition help within your church?

4. What do you have an emotional attachment to in your church or worship? Does this hinder or help in experiencing God in new ways?

5. How does your church blend heritage with innovation?

6. Has your church struggled with being led by the crowd? If so, how have you overcome this? If you are still in this situation, what can you do to change things?

7. Is your church personality-driven or mission-driven? How is this evidenced?

8. What is the mission statement of your church? How are you, personally, connected to the mission?

9. How is your church's mission statement connected to a story? How do you intentionally convey that story to new (and existing) members?

10. How are you, as a leader, working to connect people to the church's mission?

11. What steps can your church take to create a "culture of safety"? Where are you already succeeding in this area?

12. Do you wear a mask to church? How can you help create a culture of vulnerability and safety in the areas in which you lead?

TWO ★ EVERYONE IS A VIP

I have no use for people who throw their
weight around as celebrities, or for those who
fawn over you just because you are famous.

—WALT DISNEY

I f you walk around a Disney park, store, or office building you will notice one striking similarity—everyone is wearing a name tag that states the person's first name only and hometown. Bob Iger is the current CEO of the Disney Corporation. If he were to be seen walking around the Disney parks you would expect the Cast Members to address him as Mr. Iger. In the Disney culture, however, that would be highly frowned upon. He's Bob.

Disney prides itself on being a "first name company." Whether you are a janitor, an accountant, a performer, or in upper management, you are referred to by your first name. This concept, at first blush, comes across a little odd in an American culture where titles reflect power. If the average person on the street, with no understanding of the Disney culture, saw a street sweeper say, "Hi, Bob!" to the CEO of the company, the first thought would probably be, "I bet that guy is packing his bags within the hour."

To say that Disney is a first-name organization does not mean that it is chaotic or lacking in hierarchy. Far from it. Every Cast Member knows the role she or he is supposed to play in accomplishing the mission of Disney. There is definitely someone in charge and a chain of command to be followed. However, this does not mean that the "first name" concept is simply a gimmick.

Walt Disney once said, "I don't propose to be an authority on anything at all. I follow the opinions of ordinary people I meet."[1] Walt enjoyed talking to his guests and the Cast Members to find out their ideas. He didn't believe in the "top down" style of leadership, but felt that good ideas could come from anywhere.

Because Walt built the concept of looking under every rock for good ideas into the corporate culture, the top Disney executives still do it. Michael Eisner, especially early in his career, was famous for going out of his way to talk to "front-line" Cast Members. He wanted to hear from those who interacted with Disney's target audience on a daily basis. Walt always felt these Cast Members were the source of the best ideas. In speaking with various Cast Members, I've been told that Bob Iger tries to follow a similar pattern. John Lasseter, chief creative officer for Disney's Pixar branch, also continues the tradition. In a recent interview he said, "One of the most popular questions is always whether groups are more creative than individuals. My answer: In most cases, it's the team—provided you follow certain rules. As a manager, it is my task to abolish hierarchies. It doesn't matter at all who has the idea; that's a very important rule for us. The group must be honest, direct, and endeavor to sincerely help the creative individual."[2]

Let's pause for a minute of honest self-evaluation. No one can read your thoughts, so this is just between you and God. Can you honestly say within your church that it doesn't matter who comes up with a good idea? Can you honestly say that titles aren't important? Can you honestly say that the hierarchy of your church exists to resource ministry or does it function more as a gatekeeper? If you answered no to one or more of these questions, don't despair. You have a lot of company. While I don't have any research to back up the claim, from personal experience and observation I would say that 80 percent or more of churches would answer no to most, or all, of those questions. It's time for a change in how we do church, and that's what this chapter is all about.

WHAT'S IN A NAME?

Through my years of ministry I've been called a variety of things, including Brother Chris, Pastor Chris, Reverend Perry, Doctor Perry, and even a few things I can't put into print. What I'm called is usually determined by the culture of the church in which I serve. The "high church" congregations tend to prefer "Reverend" or "Doctor." The more rural people usually go with "Brother." They are all meant to show respect for the pastor, but also, often, serve to place the pastor on a pedestal. If I'm a visiting pastor I just go with it and don't make a fuss about titles. However, within my own congregation I've tried to shift the norm to just calling me "Chris." I want our church to be a "first name company" like Disney. We all know our roles, but titles aren't important. My position as pastor is no higher than the person who keeps the nursery or scrubs the toilets. This is why I insist on never being called a "minister," but more on that later.

If you're reading this as a layperson, you may struggle a little with calling your pastor by his or her first name. The idea of titles for pastors has been ingrained so much in our culture (especially in the Bible Belt) that we have difficulty in making the switch. The tradition goes well back into church history, so we're fighting an uphill battle to change something several hundred years in the making. And, to be honest, many of my clergy colleagues don't help the situation. They lap up the prestige of being called "reverend." This isn't exactly a new situation, either. In Matthew 23:6–7 Jesus says, "They love to have the place of honor at banquets and the best seats in the synagogues, and to be greeted with respect in the marketplaces, and to have people call them rabbi." You can take those exact words, put "church" in place of "synagogue" and "reverend" in place of "rabbi," and you would think Jesus spoke these words about many modern clergy.

My father, Dr. Wayne Perry, published an article in 2003 that detailed his research findings that clergy had a significantly higher need for the affirmation of others when compared to the average person.[3] This tendency towards narcissism (excessive focus on your own wants, needs, and ego) means that some pastors covet titles and have a need to be given credit for all success within the church. Often this tendency is subconscious. There are very few pastors who are aware of this tendency within themselves. I certainly don't believe most of my colleagues are intentional attention seekers. The need comes from their life experience and personality. Because this area is a blind spot for so many clergy, it is vital that they have good lay leaders to help keep that tendency in check.

There is nothing wrong with honoring your pastor. In 1 Timothy 5:17 Paul says that the elders of the church deserve "double honor," especially those who preach and teach. Jesus was also clear that when we seek public recognition we've received our reward in full (compare Matt. 6:5). So honor and respect your pastor, but help your pastor not to place him- or herself on a pedestal. Being a pastor can be a lonely position. Being responsible for the spiritual well-being of an entire church, whether that's fifty people or five thousand, is an extremely stressful job. You're blamed for not being a mind reader and for not being able to be everywhere at once. You have some people who want to tell you every problem they've ever had and others who shun you because of your position. No wonder burnout is common. Pastors need to know their hard work and sacrifice is appreciated. Honoring your pastor, however, does not mean that you view him or her as being more "spiritual" than anyone else who works hard for the cause of Christ. We're all on the same team with different roles.

As I mentioned earlier, one title I absolutely will not answer to is that of "minister." I do realize that in some cultures the term "minister" is the official title, as a good friend of mine from the United Kingdom pointed out. In this case, I am referring to the term "minister" as it is most often used in the United States—as an unofficial term. For instance, persons in the American South, especially, have a very bad habit of referring to the pastor as the "minister." That is theologically (the way we think about God) and ecclesiologically (the way we think about the church) incorrect, but functionally it is often spot on. Allow me to clarify. As a member of the clergy, I am not a "minister." I'm a pastor. Every single Christian is a minister (compare 1 Pet. 2:9, Rev. 5:10). The Protestant church fathers, especially, fought against the idea of thinking of clergy as being "above" lay Christians. Many of the ninety-five theses Martin Luther posted on the door of the church at Wittenberg on October 31, 1517, railed against the idea that people could only come to God through the priests. Luther firmly believed that everyone who trusts in Jesus is a priest (minister).[4] John Calvin said, "In him [Jesus] we are all priests."[5] John Wesley lived out the idea in founding the Methodist movement. The overwhelming majority of early Methodist pastors were laypeople, not seminary-trained, ordained clergy. If Wesley had not trusted laity then the Methodist movement would have died before ever crossing to North America.

I hope you don't hear me bashing ordained clergy. I am one, so I certainly have nothing against the idea. The point is that the pastor is not the "minister." By calling the pastor the "minister" it is implied that the pastor is the one who performs all the ministry. In practicality, this is often the case, especially in small churches. The laity comes to church so that the pastor can minister to, and on behalf of, them. This type of relationship leads to an unhealthy spiritual codependency. The laity feels they need the clergy to meet their spiritual needs and the clergy depend on the positive feedback of the laity and the feeling of being "needed" for their own sense of well-being. This relationship is completely contrary to the biblical idea.

The Bible often uses the image of the shepherd to describe the pastor. The shepherd's job was to feed and protect the sheep; to make sure the sheep were as healthy as possible. It was not the job of the shepherd to be a sheep for the sheep. To put it into church terms—my job is to spiritually feed and equip my people so that they can do the ministry, not to do the ministry for them. Rather than the pastor doing all of the teaching, all of the visitation, all of counseling, all of the planning, and so on, a successful church is one in which a person can receive a visit from any member of the church family and feel spiritually cared for just as adequately as if the pastor had visited. We are all equally important.

I am a big fan of sports, so allow me this analogy: If the church is a football team, most people would immediately think of the pastor as the quarterback—the leader, the one who gains all the glory and makes all the plays. In reality, that is the model that is in place in most churches.

However, I believe the model of Christ would make the pastor the offensive line, not the quarterback. My job is not to score the touchdowns, but to remove any obstacles and protect my people from those things that would stop them from scoring. My people are the quarterback or running back. I'm the blocker making sure Christ gets the glory through their ministry.

I hope these analogies help you to see that being a pastor is a function. It is my calling, but it is not a higher calling than yours or any other ministry among God's people and it is not a higher state of spirituality. Your calling is just as valid and holy as mine. If you want to be all that God created you to be, then ask your pastor to train and equip you, but relieve him or her of the burden of "doing" the ministry for you, which includes making the pastor solely responsible for your spiritual nourishment.

I've heard people claim they were leaving a church because they weren't "being fed." I find that very interesting because, in terms of maturity, how long do humans need someone else to feed them? By the age of two most children are capable of feeding themselves. Eventually, children will grow into adults and be able to provide their own food. As Christians we are to grow into maturity where we become responsible for our own nourishment. It's great if your pastor is a source of nourishment for you, but he or she should not carry the sole responsibility of making sure you're are being spiritually fed unless you are an infant in the faith. In my home my wife does most of the cooking, so in that regard she "feeds" me. However, I'm also capable of buying and preparing my own meals (and not just a bowl of cereal). I'm able to feed myself even though I'm often fed through the work of another because taking care of our family is part of Renae's ministry. So it should be with your spiritual life. Part of your pastor's ministry is to prepare good, healthy spiritual nourishment for you, but you also need to be able to feed yourself.

If you want to call your pastor "brother" or "reverend" go ahead. Just be sure you understand, and your pastor understands, that these are titles of respect, but not status or a higher state of spiritual existence. We're all on the same team and we're all working together to accomplish the mission of Christ. At the foot of the cross, we're all equals.

ON MISSION

I've spent the last little bit mostly talking about the relationship between laity and clergy. Many of the same issues, however, play out between the folks who sit in the pews. Have you ever seen a leader in your church who had to receive credit for every idea or who tried to control as much of the church as possible? In larger churches it's difficult for one person to control much, but you do often see groups of people engaged in power plays. Small churches, especially, have to be careful whom they allow into leadership. Those who seek leadership positions often aren't the best candidates. The Holy Spirit must play a vital role in the selection of leaders. If you're looking for someone to chair your finance committee you might find someone who wants the job and has a lot of expertise in finances but is spiritually immature. Putting this person into a position of leadership, even with his or her expertise, is asking for trouble. Instead, spend a year involving this person in a discipleship group where he or she can grow in faith and then, if ready, assume a leadership role for the right reasons. Disney is very intentional in how it brings its leaders along. They don't promote someone into a leadership position until they know that person can be trusted with the responsibility.

In the Disney family, all Cast Members understand they are dedicated to one mission: making people happy. This is expressed in a variety of ways, but everyone understands that core concept. Likewise, in the church all leaders, whether lay or clergy, must be focused on the same mission: making disciples. Matthew 28:19–20 is incredibly clear in its focus. Jesus says our mission is to make disciples. Everything else in that passage is a description of what making disciples is all about. According to the Greek, "make disciples" is the imperative verb. That's excellent because half of our job description is already written by Jesus. We know the end result of every leadership position in the church. If that position does not lend itself to making disciples then it has no place in the church.

Let's explore how this concept looks in practical terms. I'm going to use the United Methodist terminology for the various committees since that's my context, but I'm sure you can draw the parallels to whatever is called for in your church polity. In many churches, possibly most churches, the Board of Trustees exists to maintain the physical plant of the church and make policies to keep the building(s) from being abused. The trustees look at themselves as being important and entrusted with a sacred duty, which is true. Their job is very important. What if, however, the trustees took seriously the idea that every ministry in the church was as vital as their own so that their mission became to ensure that every space in the church was adequately equipped to make disciples (for example, do the Sunday school teachers have the resources they need? Does the entrance to the church create a welcoming environment?)? The difference in the focus is that it goes from being exclusive (how do we keep people from messing up our stuff) to inclusive (how do we create the most conducive atmosphere for making disciples).

Another example: In many churches the finance committee exists to set and control the budget of the church. What if, instead, the finance committee saw it as their mission to find ways to fund and resource the ministries needed by the church? The first scenario means if anyone wants to spend any money in the church, they first must sell the finance committee on the idea and convince them to write the check. At first blush you might think, "What's wrong with that? They're just being good stewards of the church's money." But, in this scenario, is the committee seeking to control or empower? Do they view the ministry of others as equally important to their own? I fully realize funds are not unlimited. But the church has a clear mission and vision, and if the ministry teams determine that a proposed ministry fits within the mission and vision of the church, then rather than acting as judge and jury on the proposal the finance committee should act as advocates, doing everything in their power to fund the request. If it's not possible, that's okay. The attitude is the concern.

A third example: In the United Methodist Church we have the Staff-Parish Relations Committee (SPRC or Pastor-Parish depending on the size of the church). This is the committee most clergy dread dealing with because usually the only time we meet with them is for our annual review and when we've done something wrong. Reviews can be done constructively, but usually they serve to tell the pastor everything he or she has done wrong. That's a little disheartening. Rarely have I walked out of an SPRC meeting feeling uplifted or empowered. The opposite extreme is equally unhealthy, which is when the SPRC is stacked with "yes-men" (and women) who just tell the pastor how wonderful he or she is. What if, instead of being a watchdog, the SPRC saw their mission as making sure their staff are as spiritually, emotionally, and physically healthy as possible so that they can fulfill the mission of making disciples? That means calling out the staff when they aren't taking care of themselves, but in a loving manner. The SPRC does need to hold the staff accountable to the mission of the church, but they don't need to call the staff on the carpet every time someone complains. If the SPRC took the role of coach, helping the staff members to be as effective and healthy as possible, instead of a watchdog, then the church would operate more effectively in every area. I'm very fortunate to have had an SPRC chair over the last couple of years who takes this attitude, and it has really opened my eyes to how the laity can be a huge asset to helping the clergy reach maximum effectiveness.

The examples I've given are just a few from my denomination. You can, and should, apply these same questions to every committee or ministry team in the local church of your denomination. Evaluate how they function, especially on the subconscious level. Do they seek to empower or control? Is every committee member trained in the mission of the church and how his or her committee helps fulfill that mission? Are leaders selected through politics or, more commonly, because they are a warm body to fill the slot, or are leaders sought, trained, and released through intentional prayer and growth? Do the people on every committee view all the ministries of the church as equally important as their own?

HONOR ALL

Another key aspect to engaging and empowering the leaders of your church is to make sure you honor them on a regular basis. Celebrate their service and achievements. This is something Disney does extremely well. When guests write e-mails or letters, or make phone calls about particular Cast Members making a positive difference in their vacations, then Disney celebrates that in front of those Cast Members' entire teams. Celebrating what they have done well makes the Cast Member being honored feel like his or her efforts are worthwhile and encourages others to strive for similar results.

Often I see situations in churches where someone has taught Sunday school or children's church for years with little to no recognition. Maybe someone has cut the church yard or fixed communion faithfully with not so much as a "thank you." One of the chief complaints I hear from churches is the lack of volunteers. Pastors often lament the "80-20 rule" (20 percent of the people doing 80 percent of the work). I don't argue the legitimacy of this claim. I've seen it in action in every church I've served. But rarely do I hear anyone discussing why this is the case. I think part of the reason is that workers are undertrained and underappreciated.

When I was fifteen I took a job at Burger King. On my first day of work two people called in sick, leaving us shorthanded. I was placed on the burger line making Whoppers with only about a five-minute explanation of what to do. To say that I felt overwhelmed and frustrated would be a huge understatement. I almost quit that first day. This scenario is what we often do to our workers in the church. We ask them to fill a position and then we throw them into the fire with little training—just a "good luck" and a pat on the back. Most people want to faithfully serve God so they do their best, but with minimal training and resources they flounder until they are able to get out of the commitment. Next time they are asked to serve in a position they are more than likely going to refuse.

The other reason we often have trouble with volunteers is that people don't feel important. They feel like all the hard work they do isn't valued. Clergy Appreciation Month is celebrated every October, but how often do we celebrate the volunteers within the church? Any church that wants to have an abundance of volunteers will build celebration into its culture. People like success stories. Doing a two- or three-minute video or a live interview a couple of times a month that celebrates the ministry of someone in the church will do wonders for the volunteer pool. It doesn't take a lot of time or effort but makes a tremendous impact. If you are on a committee or ministry team, especially if you're the chairperson, take time to write a note of appreciation every so often to the other team members. It doesn't take much. A simple "I appreciate all the hard work you put in with this team" will make a person feel that maybe her or his effort is worthwhile after all. And if you can show people specific ways that their ministry is advancing God's realm and helping change lives then you'll never need to worry about burnout.

Let me pause for a moment here to say that I don't really like the word "volunteer." There are two reasons: First, "volunteer" implies that we have some say-so in the matter. I am choosing to do this as opposed to recognizing that God has called me to this ministry. Second, we often ask people to volunteer for menial tasks, especially those no one really wants to do, rather than recruiting missionaries/ministers/partners/teammates to join in the world-changing vision and mission of Christ. There's a big difference in those two attitudes. So, though I used the word "volunteer" in the previous paragraph because it's the one most commonly used in the church, I want to challenge you to rethink your word use. By using a different term, you might convey what you're actually calling people to accomplish.

Sharing the stories of those in ministry within your church is also a way to continue to emphasize the church's mission. By showing these stories on a regular basis you are hammering home the message of "This is what we value; this is why we're here" to everyone sitting in the pews. People will rush to be a part of something they see as important. For instance, after the September 11, 2001, terrorist attacks, the military recruiting offices were overwhelmed by the number of new volunteers. Men and women who had never previously considered military service suddenly wanted to do their part for their country because their story connected to what happened in New York City and Washington, D.C. If you help your people to see the need and the value then you'll never have to beg for volunteers again. Honor every person who serves in your church. Celebrate each one's ministry and they will all be happy to continue doing that ministry.

POWER PLAYS

It is an unfortunate reality that some people get into church leadership for the wrong reasons. Some clergy and laity serve out of self-need, desire for control, or desire for prestige. How do you handle these situations? The ideal is to never let them into a leadership position at all, but sometimes people slip through the cracks or they act one way beforehand, but once in a leadership position they take on a different persona.

Disney has had to deal with its share of power plays, too. It's something that will happen when very creative and passionate people get together. When the Pixar team first came together to do *Toy Story*, they were being micromanaged and "bullied" by Jeffrey Katzenberg, then head of Walt Disney Studios. Katzenberg insisted on having the characters and story of *Toy Story* fit his ideas, which meant overriding the team that had developed the original concept. Eventually, John Lasseter (CEO of Pixar) and his team stood up to the "bully" and went with their own vision. Their vision of *Toy Story* is now one of the most loved stories in the Disney movie library. The Pixar team won the day by working together to accomplish their goal and by not allowing the power play to derail their vision.[6]

Power plays are something all church leaders will have to deal with at some point. I mentioned earlier how deadly power plays can be to achieving the overall mission of the church, so it is vital that you understand how to deal with them. I mentioned one way, above, as the Pixar team united against the power play attempt. There is strength in unity, and that will often put an end to power plays. Of course, Disney also has the luxury of simply firing someone if they refuse to play nice. In the church, we often do not have that option available to us, so learning how to manage a power play is vital to church leadership.

The first step is to have strong leadership in place. In most cases where I have seen power struggles become a real problem it was usually due to there being only one or two strong leaders in the group, if any. When you have two strong leaders and the rest are weak, then you have an ideal set up for an "alpha dog" struggle. This situation often arises in smaller churches where the pool of potential leaders is limited and sometimes the nominations committee is just looking for a warm body to fill a position required by the denominational structure.

In order to combat this situation, make sure you are careful in selecting your leaders each year. You can't have an off year for leadership. No matter how tempting it is, the qualifications for being in a leadership position must extend beyond having a pulse. If you don't feel that you have enough qualified persons to fill the positions required, then modify your structure, if possible, or speak with your denominational hierarchy to look for another solution. When a person with a tendency toward control and power plays sees that the other leaders on their team are also strong, then that person will usually settle down and play nice. Or quit. Either way, you win.

A second way to help prevent power struggles is to model idea sharing and valuing each team member. When all persons have a chance to be heard, no matter how far-fetched their ideas may seem, they will usually feel less of a need to seize control. A large number of power grabs come from people who feel that their ideas won't be heard any other way. Even if you know you won't use an idea in a million years, just taking the time to listen will make the person expressing the idea feel valued and a part of the team.

Third, make sure you have checks and balances within your church system. If you know person X is particularly strong willed, though a capable leader, make sure he or she serves on a committee with others who won't roll over for them. Also, make sure no one committee within your church structure can overrule all the rest. For instance, in the United Methodist system the SPRC sets the pastor's salary. The finance committee, however, also has a say, and the eventual approval has to go before the entire charge conference. In this manner we don't have one committee either blowing the church's budget by overpaying the pastor (rarely an issue) or creating an unfair situation for the pastor because one or two very stingy people find their way onto the SPRC.

One of the great complaints about a system of checks and balances is that nothing is ever accomplished. This is the big issue with the American government. If one party controls the presidency and another controls one, or both, houses of Congress, then we can end up with a stalemate where nothing is ever accomplished. If your church is all about personal agendas and power, the same thing will happen. In fact, if you see very little happening in your church, you might examine that very issue. However, I firmly believe that if we are all focused on the mission of Christ, then we will work together, instead of opposing each other. In that case, a system of checks and balances will help us to test the direction we're going as Scripture instructs (see, for instance, Acts 17:11 and 1 John 4:1).

What if a power struggle does erupt? A statement that should be obvious is to act in a Christ-like manner. The key word is "should." Often when power struggles happen the parties involved are more focused on self-interests than those of Christ. As the old adage goes, "When you are up to your neck in alligators, it's hard to remember that the original goal was to drain the swamp!" This is a situation where laypersons can be of invaluable assistance to the pastor.

If a pastor steps into a power struggle, there are a couple of likely outcomes, neither of them positive. First, both parties could turn against the pastor, seeing the pastor's involvement as a threat to their power. Or one or both parties could see the pastor as taking sides on the issue, which could lead to a bigger blowup. Both scenarios can happen even if the pastor acts with perfect motives and leadership skill. If, on the other hand, a respected lay leader helps mediate the conflict, often things can be resolved quicker. For some reason pastors seem to be lightning rods for emotional reactions. Exactly why, I don't know, but the best thing a pastor can do in this situation is to rely on his or her strong leaders to help work through it.

So, back to my initial statement: act in a Christ-like manner. What does that mean? Jesus reminds us that we cannot truly worship God when we are in open conflict with someone (Matt. 5:23–24). We must, for the sake of the spiritual atmosphere within the church, resolve the conflict as quickly as possible. Do not wait and see if it all works out. Be proactive.

Part of being proactive means to pray before doing anything else. Resolving a power struggle within the church is one of the most difficult tasks a leader can face. Both sides might feel that they are entirely in the right, that God is on their side alone, and they will be extremely invested emotionally. Taking on this task is truly walking into the lion's den and therefore unwise to handle without a lot of prayer.

Step two is to make sure you have your own motives and attitude straight before attempting to help anyone else. Paul tells us in Romans 12:17, "Do not repay anyone evil for evil, but take thought for what is noble in the sight of all." And Jesus says in Matthew 7:4–5, "Or how can you say to your neighbor, 'Let me take the speck out of your eye,' while the log is in your own eye? You hypocrite, first take the log out of your own eye, and then you will see clearly to take the speck out of your neighbor's eye." In other words, you must be right with God before you can approach anyone else. I don't think you can accomplish this completely on your own. You need a trusted friend (not a spouse) who will be completely honest with you in doing this evaluation. Pick someone who will speak the truth in love and help you work through any issues you need to address.

Once you are sure of your own heart, follow the advice of Christ in Matthew 18:15–17. Jesus tells us to first go to the person one on one. If the person won't listen, then bring a couple of others with us. If the person still won't listen, then we bring it up before the entire church. This provides the perfect model. If you go to someone one on one, you save that person embarrassment and allow him or her to adjust. If the person's heart remains hard, then you still keep it within a small group. Only after that fails do you bring in the pastor and other "official" church leaders. If you reach this stage, more than likely only something major will change the person anyway. If you start off privately then you can save the individiual's dignity and leadership ability.

THE "LEAST" ARE VIPS

Up to this point we've discussed the "everyone is important" theme in terms of the leadership of the church. Now let's explore how the leadership applies this principle to those they serve. Jesus says, in Matthew 25:40, that whatever is done to the "least" on earth is done to him. In this instance he is referring to the poor, sick and disabled, and those in prison. Disney does a wonderful job of intentionally making the "least" feel important while they are in the Disney parks. Let me say that the term "least" is not meant in any derogatory way. Jesus certainly did not mean it in that manner. When I say the "least" I am referring to those who are not considered to be at the top of our societal structure, but whom the church should view as VIPs.

In May 2006 my oldest son, Caleb, was diagnosed with type-1 diabetes. He had been to Disney World on two previous trips, but we wondered if this disease was the end of our vacation ability. We did not see how we could possibly go to a place like Disney World and manage Caleb's diabetes. When we started thinking about our next trip I mentioned this issue to a Cast Member. She put me through to a special diets' Cast Member, who was able to send me quite a lot of information on how to help Caleb during our trip. Also, the Cast Member noted Caleb's issue on our dinner reservations, and at every sit-down meal the chef personally came to our table to make sure that Caleb found something he could eat. If we weren't sold on Disney before that experience, we certainly were afterward! Since then we've made a couple of more trips and don't need the chef to come out anymore, but the fact that they were willing to go that extra mile to help my son made a huge difference in my ability to relax and enjoy our vacation.

My situation is definitely not unique. I see people with all kinds of disabilities enjoying themselves at Disney World. I spoke on the Intercot message board recently to a mother whose son is severely autistic. She commented that she never dreamed that going to Disney World would be possible, but through the helpful Cast Members and the Guest Assistance Card (a card that lets the Cast Members know someone needs extra assistance) their dream came true. While at the Disney parks people with special issues can't feel completely "normal"—it's not as if their issues go away—but they can come very close because Disney intentionally goes out of the way to make everything as accessible as possible to every person.

On the "Disney Driven Life" blog, I read a story of a family visiting Walt Disney World (WDW) with a severely autistic child: "Upon their first trip to Disney with Josh, Ray and Rachel witnessed something extraordinary—something that some parents of autistic kids wait a lifetime to see. He connected. 'He recognized the characters in the parks,' Rachel explains, 'And for whatever reason it encouraged him to speak. He made more of an effort to express himself.'" The magic of Disney in dealing with the "least" of our world is expressed in a story told by Rachel (the mom). They took their son, Josh, to the Epcot Character Connection where guests are able to meet several characters at one time. The family had no clue how their son would react to the situation. Normally the Character Connection is very noisy and can be quite overwhelming even for "normal" children. For that matter, it can be pretty overwhelming for the parents! This knowledge led to a great deal of anxiety for Rachel and her husband. They didn't want their son to miss the characters, but they didn't want him to have a meltdown either. Here's what happened: "They quietly informed the Cast Member who supervised the line that Josh was autistic. 'Everyone, may I please have your attention,' the Cast Member bellowed to the crowd, 'We have a very important person with us today, and he will need a little extra time with the characters. We know that you understand the magnitude of our special guest's visit and are so thankful for your patience.' The guests in line looked at Josh, smiled warmly, and visibly relaxed. 'Mickey! Minnie! We have a lover,' the Cast Member announced. Mickey, all his friends, and even the photographer nodded in understanding. The whole atmosphere immediately took on a more calm pace as opposed to the common assembly line feel at the Character Connection."[7]

The Cast Members were able to pull off this magic for the family because Disney has been intentional about training their Cast Members in how to make a vacation better for these special guests. One Cast Member told me that meeting "special" guests was the greatest part of her job. She said, "These kids have to struggle every day of their lives to do things other people take for granted. I will do everything I can to make sure their time here is as magical as possible."

Disney has become so well known for their accessibility to those with special needs that several websites have sprung up to help families know how to take advantage of what's available. The family I mentioned previously runs a website called WDW Autism. Disney fan sites such as Intercot and All Ears also have sections devoted to special needs, as do most all of the fan sites these days.[8] Disney reads the comments on these various sites and uses the information they gain to help make the experience for their "special" guests better.

It's one thing to teach your Cast Members how to interact with guests with special needs. It's a whole other game when you start investing money in a project. Disney's true commitment to special needs guests is shown in how much time and money they invest in making the stay of those guests more accessible. Yes, Disney does the traditional ramps and wider doorways to help out, but where they stand out, many guests may never notice. One of my favorite bits of technology is used for the deaf community. In the back of all of their shows, Disney has now installed LED marquees that display all of the announcements, words, and lyrics backwards (mirror image). This enables a person to use a small pocket mirror to read the words without having to put an interpreter up on stage or requiring deaf people to sit in a certain section. Now they can sit anywhere and use a small mirror to see all of the lyrics without being distracted themselves, or distracting others. Disney Imagineers have also invented an Assistive Technology Device (ATD) for guests with vision impairment. According to the Disney Parks Blog, the device will "provide detailed descriptions of outdoor areas for visually impaired guests. Using an interactive audio menu, guests can choose the type of information they'd like to receive, from architectural elements to the location of the nearest restroom. It works using wireless technology to pinpoint its location and take preprogrammed actions. Best of all, it fits in the palm of your hand."[9] The ATD also amplifies show lyrics and words for guests with hearing impairment. Mark Jones, the manager of services for guests with disabilities, shares another example: "There were no official signs in American Sign Language for Disney characters and locations, so in 1996, the Walt Disney Company created some official signs to be incorporated into many of the interpreted performances in the parks. They worked with guests and professional interpreters to find out which signs were the most logical and intuitive based on the characters and locations."[10] The true priorities of a company are shown by where they spend their time and money. They can claim all they want that they care about special needs guests, but when they start investing large amounts of time and money then you know those claims are more than just talk.

As already noted, Jesus commands his followers to reach out to the "least" of the world. How well does your church accomplish this mission? Does your church claim to be a place for all people? Does it actually put its money towards making that claim become a reality? I would strongly encourage your church to do an accessibility audit.[11] By auditing your church you go beyond subjective thinking and force yourselves to take a hard look at how well you are backing up your claims.

The physical plant is important, but you also need to audit the ministries and attitudes of your church. Are the ministries of your church accessible to the visually and hearing impaired? Would an autistic child be welcomed and ministered to in your Sunday school or children's church? Would your nursery workers and teachers know how to interact with a special needs child?

Most churches can't be prepared for every eventuality. You may not have the staff or budget to meet the needs of every special needs person, but if the attitude of the church is one of openness, welcoming, and love, then you can overcome most of the barriers. The key is to make sure that you are sensitive to the needs of the "least," which is who Jesus deemed to be VIPs in God's kingdom, or realm.

NOTICE THE LITTLE ONES

Special needs persons aren't the only population that requires special attention. In Matthew 19:14 Jesus commands his followers to let the children have access to him. Jesus always made time for the little ones. Many churches take on the attitude that children should be "seen and not heard," which seems contrary to the attitude of Christ. Going against something Jesus specifically said is not a very good idea for any Christian, so we need to examine how we can better minister to our children.

If I told you that the Disney parks excel at reaching children, your first response would probably be, "Thanks for that brilliant observation. Next I suppose you'll tell us the sky is blue." The reason Disney excels at reaching children is not, however, what you might think. Other theme parks have tried introducing characters and child-centered rides without the success of Disney. So where do they fall short?

The first place to notice Disney's passion for children is to go into the restrooms. Every restroom has child-sized sinks and toilets. This may seem an inconsequential detail, but if you claim that children are important then children should find things designed specifically for them. Another example is to walk along Main St. USA in the Magic Kingdom. The buildings are represented as being three stories tall, but actually they use a forced perspective technique. Walt wanted the buildings to have the feel of grandeur, but he didn't want them to actually be so big that they overwhelmed the children. So each "story" is actually smaller than the previous, but because of the perspective of looking up it still "feels" three stories without feeling overwhelming. Cast Members are often told to get down on their knees when looking around the park so as to get a child's perspective when looking for sight lines, trash, or repairs that are needed. The executives, especially, spend a lot of time looking at the parks from the child's perspective. Finally, look at how the characters interact with the children. Most of the characters are six feet tall (or more). That can seem overwhelming to many adults. When a small child approaches, the characters almost always kneel down to be on the child's level. By coming down to the child's level, as opposed to having the parent pick the child up, Mickey and friends become a lot less intimidating and are seen as friends, not "grown-ups."

I could give many more examples of how Disney intentionally shows children that they are important, but I think you get the gist of the idea. All of these ideas I've mentioned involve intentional training and/or planning. Child-size sinks didn't accidently appear in the bathrooms. The characters don't all instinctively know to kneel down when a child approaches. Yes, Disney knows that children are their bread and butter. If they lose the children they go out of business. However, they go way above and beyond in making children feel special. Even something so simple as giving a child an "It's My Birthday" button when a child visits the park on his or her birthday can make the child feel very special.

How do you make children feel special in your church? Or do you? Do they feel like they truly matter at your church or are they an afterthought? Are children ministered to at their level or are they told to just "sit and listen"? Do the facilities at your church tell children they are important? Does your church budget reflect the importance of children? As mentioned previously, we can say a ministry is important, but until we devote funds to that ministry, our words are simply giving lip service.

Many of the techniques Disney uses to make children feel special would work in your church context as well. Kneel down when a child is speaking to you. Have special "It's My Birthday" buttons that you can give on children's birthdays. Teach them using techniques that will make the Bible come alive for them as opposed to just feeding them information or expecting them to grasp what is being taught to the adults. Most importantly, involve children in ministry.

No child is too young to minister in Jesus' name. Often we're only willing to allow children to minister in roles specifically designated for children, such as acolytes, children's choir, or being the "teacher's helper" in Sunday school. Those things are great, but they teach children their ministry is only valuable in that context and not in doing "real" ministry. I allow some of the older children in my church to serve as lay readers, which means they sit beside me during Sunday worship and read the Scripture selections for the day just as adults do. I have children being greeters on Sunday. Children assist in handing out food at the soup kitchen we participate in and in our monthly Angel Food Ministry distribution.[12] In each of these cases and others, the children minister alongside adults. They aren't shunted aside or patted on the head for their efforts, but allowed to do the same ministry the adults do. This is not possible in every ministry, certainly, but by allowing children to minister with adults we show them that they can be valuable in service to Christ now and not just when they are adults.

Walt Disney, specifically, didn't want the Disney brand to just be about children. He wanted it to be about children and adults being able to do things together. Marty Skyler worked directly with Walt Disney for many years and recently spoke about how Disneyland came about because Walt wanted a place he could take his own children. "Absolutely, in fact he made that very clear that Disneyland came from his experiences of taking Diane and Sharon, his two daughters, to amusement parks, particularly a little amusement park at Beverly Boulevard and La Cienga Boulevard, where the Beverly Center is now—a big development in Los Angeles. He said he would have to sit on the park bench and eat peanuts or popcorn while the girls had all the fun. He started thinking, why isn't there someplace where children and their parents can have fun together?"[13]

I have always wondered why the church doesn't understand Walt's inspiration. The model for children's ministry in most churches is to separate the children from adults. We have age-level Sunday school or children's church, and age appropriate ministries for children during our various other Bible study and ministry times. It is wonderful to minister to children at their level, and very necessary, but when do children get to interact with adults in the life of the church? Teaching a child about worship and the Bible is great, but nothing will impact a child more permanently than seeing his or her parents worshiping God. Somehow the idea has arisen that in order for the adults to fully worship God the children must be removed. We tell children that they are an important part of the community of faith, yet whenever the community of faith is doing anything we separate the children out.

One church that has done a marvelous job of addressing this issue is North Point Community Church.[14] North Point was founded in the suburbs of Atlanta, Georgia, by Andy Stanley. The fledgling church struggled with how to include children in worship. Out of that struggle emerged the ministry KidStuf, a forty-five-minute worship service designed for children and parents to attend together. It is held once a month and is interactive and "fun," but intentionally designed to help parents share "God's big ideas" with their kids. North Point has plenty of age-targeted ministries for children, but they intentionally set aside time for families to be together.

Walt Disney strongly felt, and Andy Stanley echoed the idea when founding North Point, that families spend too much time apart. This idea has never been truer than in today's culture where dual-income and single-parent homes are much more common and where adults often work fifty- to sixty-hour work weeks.[15] Between work, homework, school, watching television, and extracurricular activities, parents and kids hardly interact with each other at all during a normal week. Several studies have proven this point. A study out of the University of Texas documents that the increased amount of television children watch in today's culture has, not surprisingly, had an extremely negative impact on the child's interaction with parents and siblings.[16] Dr. Wade Horn also writes, "Parents today spend roughly 40 percent less time with their children than did parents a generation ago. According to one survey, in 1965, parents spent on average about 30 hours per week with their kids. By 1985, parent-child interaction had dropped to just 17 hours per week. Another study found that almost 20 percent of children in grades six through 12 had not had a good conversation lasting for at least 10 minutes with at least one of their parents in more than a month. A poll for the National Parenting Association found that 36 percent of parents do not give any time to their kids' extracurricular activities."[17] Since further studies have shown that the amount of interaction a child has with a parent is often directly related to the child's later success in life,[18] why would we continue this problem at church?

How well does your church bring children and adults together? As we've just shown, this is an entirely different question than asking, "How well do we minister to children?" You might have the best children's ministry in the world, but it is equally important that children worship and minister alongside their parents and other adults. I previously mentioned some ways to plug children into ministry. Most of those were specific to my local situation, but you can find similar ways to plug children in. You might or might not have the resources to pull off something like KidStuf, but with some creative thought and intentional effort you can find ways for adults and children to be a part of the community of faith together.

CONCLUSION

Throughout this chapter I've covered a lot of generalities. An entire book could be written (and many have) on the various topics covered: children's ministry, special needs ministry, conflict resolution, and so on. The point of this chapter was not to give you a detailed guide on how to accomplish all of these things but to shift your mindset towards realizing the value of every person within your church and in the community around you. If you're truly interested in furthering these ministries, there are resources to help you. However, none of these things can happen until you fully embrace the idea that, in the words of Bob the Tomato of Veggie Tales fame, "God made you special and he loves you very much."[19] You are special and everyone around you is special. With that attitude, you can minister the way Jesus did.

★

LIVING INTO THE LESSON

1. How do you feel personally about Disney's first name policy? Does it make you feel more or less comfortable in a professional setting? How about in a church setting?

2. How would this kind of attitude function at your church?

3. How would the idea that we are all the "ministers" change the way your church functions?

4. How does being "fed" versus finding your own nourishment play out in your church family? Is it a balance or does one outweigh the other?

5. How do the leadership teams in your church function? Are they seeking to empower or control?

6. How often do you celebrate those who minister within your church?

7. How has your church handled power struggles successfully, or not so successfully, in the past? How can you handle this better in the future?

8. How is your church equipped to handle people with special needs? In which areas can you improve readiness and accessibility?

9. How does your church intentionally seek to minister to children? Are children allowed to participate in ministry within your church? Why or why not?

10. How does your church bring parents and children together in worship in ministry? Where can you intentionally seek to bring families together?

THREE ★ BLUE SKY THINKING

All our dreams can come true,
if we have the courage to pursue them.

—WALT DISNEY

If there is one thing Walt Disney Imagineering is known for, it's the Blue Sky process. The Blue Sky process is where all the rides and other creations begin. At that point there are no rules, no barriers, just endless possibilities. Too often in the church we look at every idea to see if we have the budget or workforce—whether staff or volunteers—to make it happen. If not, we dismiss it immediately. By learning to embrace the Blue Sky process, church leaders can learn to unleash infinite possibilities for ministry. It's the difference between looking at a problem and asking, "Why?" instead of, "Why not?"

DARE TO DREAM

Marty Skylar, executive vice president and ambassador for Walt Disney Imagineering until his retirement in 2009, describes the Blue Sky process like this: "There are two ways to look at a blank sheet of paper. One way is to see it as the most frightening thing in the world because when you're faced with that blank page, you must make the first mark on it. It doesn't matter whether you're an artist, a writer, an engineer, or an accountant. Making that first mark is the challenge. The other way to look at that blank sheet of paper is to see it as the greatest opportunity in the world. . . . You can let your imagination fly in any direction."[1]

I certainly identify with Marty's statement. Whether I'm writing this book, a sermon, notes for Bible study, or any other project, I have found the hardest words to write to be the first ones on the page. Staring at the blank sheet is thrilling and terrifying at the same time. Walt Disney is famous for saying, "If you can dream it, you can do it."[2] That's true, but for many of us it's easier said than done. We humans tend to be a scared bunch and approach dreams much like Marty's first scenario: with fear. We can dream, but we can also come up with infinite reasons as to why that dream is impossible. We end up talking ourselves out of the dream before we ever pursue it.

Walt's mantra of "dream, believe, dare, do" is vital to our success as a church. It all starts with dreams. Then we have to believe the dream is possible, dare to attempt it, and do it. But it all starts with the dream. That's where Blue Sky thinking will help us most. In Blue Sky thinking we learn to forget about limitations and dream big. I was once told that every Christian needs a Big, Hairy, Audacious God-goal (BHAG). A BHAG is something so big that without God in it we'll fall flat on our face. If we're not chasing a BHAG then we're not really living by faith. How many churches and individual Christians are living life focused on a BHAG? I'd wager that the vast majority of us focus on goals we know we can accomplish with our own strength and resources, which usually isn't much.

The people who have accomplished the most throughout history have been the biggest dreamers. Martin Luther King Jr. told the whole world that he had a dream,[3] even though many at the time thought that dream was impossible. When Lance Armstrong was diagnosed with cancer, he dreamed of winning a Tour de France even though his doctors told him that he probably wouldn't live more than another few months. Christopher Columbus dreamed of finding a new passage to India by sailing west even though his contemporaries thought he was crazy. Bill Gates dreamed of a computer in every home during a time when computers filled entire rooms with less computing power than is now on my cell phone. And Walt Disney set out from his Missouri home for Hollywood with only $40 and a dream of starting his own studio. Without big dreams we never would have heard of any of these people.

How many folks are sitting in your pews with a big dream feeling like they'll never achieve it? Paul writes in Philippians 4:13 that we can accomplish anything through the strength of Christ, yet we tend to focus on our own human frailties. Does your church have an intentional process for unlocking and unleashing the dreams of those in your community of faith?

Bill Capodagli and Lynn Jackson, when trying to explain Pixar's amazing success, wrote, "When we were children the truth lived in our imaginations—where we were the princess in the castle or the knights in shining armor slaying the dragon. In our minds, we could do anything! But then parents, teachers, and bosses chased the little kid right out of us. Dreaming, making believe, acting impulsively, and taking risks were not rewarded in the "real world"—the adult world."[4]

Bob Iger wrote, "Five decades ago, there was simply nowhere on Earth where one could find a full-time group of creative and innovative individuals whose job was to imagine, design, and create three-dimensional, living stories."[5] Bob is touting the uniqueness of Walt Disney Imagineering, but as I read his words I thought, "That's what the church is supposed to be!" The community of faith should be a full-time (in lifestyle, not necessarily in pay) group of creative and innovative individuals unleashing living, breathing three-dimensional stories. Every person in our church is a living story. Every person has a faith story to share. Part of our job as church leaders is to help connect those individual stories to the meta-narrative (God's story) and then help them live out their stories as examples of God's grace in the world.

Bob used two key words, however, that are usually not associated with the church: creative and innovative. The church is generally woefully behind the culture. What is generally accepted as "contemporary" worship in today's churches is stylistically from the 1970s. Even the most "cutting-edge" worship style right now dates to the 1990s. This may shock you, but I don't have a big problem with that. Cultural fads change very quickly. The church should not be running to keep up with cultural fads in the way we do worship. I think many churches spend way too much time fighting worship wars when any style you choose is probably already outdated and irrelevant in today's culture anyway. People want real substance. They want to see how their story connects to God's story, but I have seen very little evidence that the method of worship matters. I realize that every individual has a preference, but in terms of being able to attract people to your church, the style of worship is one of the least important factors. If you do a good job with contemporary worship, people will like it. If you do a good job with traditional worship, however, people are going to like that, too. Adam Hamilton has grown one of the largest churches in the United States outside of Kansas City, Missouri, through mostly traditional worship.

If worship style doesn't matter to the general populace all that much, then what does matter? The important point is that we creatively engage the issues presented in our culture. We provide a solid foundation for people to stand on in an ever shifting culture. "Contemporary" worship does not have a corner on the creative market and "traditional" worship is not the only place people can find substance. It's all in how we approach the issues.

Disney World and Disneyland both have a section called Tomorrowland. When Disneyland first opened in 1955, Tomorrowland was supposed to be a way to showcase Walt's tremendous optimism in the future. This optimism was most clear in the Carousel of Progress. On this attraction the audience followed a family from the late 1800s through the technological advances of the twentieth century, ending with a look into a very optimistic future and how technology would make our lives better. The theme song proudly proclaims, "There's a Great Big Beautiful Tomorrow."

In the midst of all of this optimism, the Imagineers faced a problem. How could they create a vision of the future that wasn't outdated before it opened? The rate of change in our culture since the beginning of the twentieth century is staggering. If you look at how slowly innovation happened in the world up until the late 1800s, then looking at the 1900s would make your head spin. And things aren't slowing down. There's a big difference, though. In our postmodern culture, technology is no longer seen as the savior of the future. Jeff Kurti, Disney historian, writes, "The sad reality was that technology was not a savior and much of the advancement anticipated during the 1950s and 1960s had pushed people further apart instead of bringing them together."[6]

To address these problems, the Imagineers constantly tried to update Tomorrowland. They were investing vast amounts of resources trying to keep pace with an ever changing society that had lost faith in technology. Finally, they decided enough was enough. They needed to quit trying to stay ahead of the curve and, instead, celebrate what they did best. They decided to completely reinvent Tomorrowland based on the dreams and ideals of the past. It has taken on a retro feel, drawing from the Buck Rodgers–style comics of the 1940s and 1950s. Instead of constantly trying to stay ahead, they celebrate the stories of the past and present them in creative and fun ways. This "retro" feel still very much connects with both the parents and grandparents who originally lived through those times as well as the kids who are experiencing it for the first time.

This provides a good lesson for the church. We need to celebrate what we do best. We should not live in the past, but use it. If your church is always trying to catch up to the latest and greatest fad to come along, then you, like Disney, will spend a lot of time and energy constantly reinventing yourself. Your people will never have a clear idea of who you are or where you're going and you'll end up controlled by the rapidly changing currents of culture instead of the Spirit of God. The fact is, the church will never be seen as "cool" or "edgy" by popular culture, regardless of how slick our pastor's goatee is or how much the praise band rocks.

Should we, then, resign ourselves to irrelevance? Of course not! The key, though, is not to try to keep up with the culture. Instead, figure out who you are as a community of faith and then come together to plan how to creatively use that identity to engage the culture with the message of Christ. As I mentioned in chapter 1, my current church does not have a lot of resources or a big building so we decided to concentrate on being friendly and welcoming to every person. We are constantly looking for ways to creatively say, "You are welcome here" to the community. That ranges from having a free yard sale, to participating in the Angel Food Ministry program, to working with a local mentally/physically handicapped group home to keep the home in good shape.

BLUE SKY PROCESS

The Blue Sky process always has to start with a dream, as we've just discussed. But, once the dream is there, what do we do with it? This section will outline how to get a Blue Sky group going in your church so that you can unleash the dreamers around you.

The first step may be one of the hardest for a church. It's to ask "what if?" instead of "what?" or "why?" Bill Capodagli says that the Blue Sky process is learning "to live for a time with the discomfort of not knowing, or not being in full control."[7] Before we even get to the church, let's start with you. When you are trying to determine what God wants you to do, do you ask "what?" or "what if?" Do you start by taking an inventory of your strengths and weaknesses and tell God, "Here's all I have to offer?" Or do you allow yourself to dream, trusting that, whatever God calls you to do, God will provide the resources necessary to accomplish the task? Your mindset makes all the difference. In the former, you can only accomplish what you personally have the strength and talent to do. In the latter, nothing is impossible. It is this latter mindset that defines the Blue Sky process. The Imagineers don't say, "We have x amount of money and x amount of time, so what can we do with that?" They say, "What if?" So let me ask, what if you lived your life with a "what if" attitude? How would that mindset change how you approach your work, your faith, and your relationships?

Now let's carry this same attitude over to the church. Does your church tend to approach ministry with a "what" or a "what if" attitude? When someone presents a new ministry idea, is the first reaction to see if you can afford it or to ask, "What if we did this?" This really is a matter of faith. Capodagli perfectly described the life of faith when he spoke of learning to live with the discomfort of not being in control. I, personally, tend to be a bit of a control freak. I like things very well ordered and my personal inclination is to have all my ducks in a row before moving on anything. From personal observation, the vast majority of churches function in the same manner. Having a controlling attitude is completely contrary to a successful life of faith, as well as successfully navigating the Blue Sky process.

So maybe we say step one in the Blue Sky process is to let go of the need for control. I'm not suggesting you suddenly turn reckless or throw wisdom out the window. The Blue Sky portion of planning is not the final product. It is simply the starting line. Eventually you do have to discuss things like budget and human resources requirements, but that time is not now. The Blue Sky time is for unleashing your dreams. If you start with your own perceived resources then you'll never become creative. You'll always play it safe. It is amazing how resources can be found when people truly buy into a dream. Suddenly something that seemed far-fetched becomes possible because when people truly believe in something they will find creative and innovate solutions to make it happen.

Set aside some time for dreaming, both in your personal life and in your church. At this point don't worry about the details, the "what." Instead, let your mind flow to the "what if." Let God's Spirit lead you wherever. Start by focusing on "What if I fully let God lead me? What if I truly buy into the idea that I can do anything in the power of Christ? How would my life and my church be different if I lived 100 percent by faith? What if I stepped out and did this ministry that I keep dreaming about even though I can't see how it could possibly happen." The slogan for Disney Parks is "Where dreams come true." If you will live your life asking these questions, and if your church will commit to this attitude, then you will find that your life *and* your church become the places where dreams come true.

ONCE UPON A TIME

Once you have committed yourself to the Blue Sky attitude, the next step in the process is to find the story. Every great Disney experience begins with a great story, whether it's a classic fairy tale, or one of the Disney cartoons, or an event from history. The point is to find the story. At Disney's Animal Kingdom you can ride Dinosaur. It's a unique and fun, dark ride, but what makes it fun are not the bumps and the speed. The entire ride is built around the story that you are being sent back in time to bring back a "friendly" dinosaur to the present. Along the way you find some thrills and chills but the story makes the ride infinitely more effective than if you were simply riding through a dark area looking at dinosaur animatronics.

Another example, Test Track, takes the guest on an interactive tour of what tests a car is put through before being allowed on the road. I mentioned previously how Rock 'n' Roller Coaster sets up the idea of taking a limo through LA rush hour traffic. Two of Disney's most famous rides, the Haunted Mansion and Pirates of the Caribbean, are completely story based. But it's not just the rides where you find stories. The '50s Prime Time Café in Disney's Hollywood Studios takes the guests back to an idealized 1950s America with your "mom" or "cousin" serving you instead of a waiter or waitress. The Indiana Jones Epic Stunt Spectacular, instead of simply being a collection of scenes from the Indiana Jones series, creates the story of shooting the movies with guests getting a backstage look at how stunts are created on the set. I could go on and describe almost every experience in the Disney resorts, whether we're talking about rides, restaurants, or hotels. Every place has a story. "Imagineers search for a story, or part of a story, that can be told experientially and in three dimensions."[8]

If you want your ministry idea to be successful, you must attach it to a story. The good news is that you won't have to search far. The life of Jesus is often called "the greatest story ever told." When you pick up a Bible, you hold in your hands the metanarrative, the ultimate story . . . God's story. That's the story everyone wants to be a part of. Your job as the local body of Christ is to connect each individual's story to God's story. If you want a ministry to go over well, don't tell people how much it will cost or how many people can get involved in it. Tell them stories of lives that are being changed, or will be changed, by this ministry. If it's something already in existence that you're trying to grow, then show and tell the stories of those who have been impacted by the ministry. Celebrate those victories and tell their stories every chance you get. If it's a new ministry, then find the stories of those in need. It's amazing how money becomes a nonissue for most people when they are sold on the need. Stories are how people connect to the need. Stories give hospitality, a place where people can feel a part of something. People can come in, wander around, and feel comfortable at every turn, because this story is part of them, even if it's a new story.

THE DEEP DIVE

A key component to making any ministry successful is to make it immersive. You do not want something that people simply volunteer for. One of my mentors once told me that when people volunteer, they retain control. It's still about them and what they are "sacrificing" for this ministry. Instead, you want people so immersed in what they are doing that it becomes their passion. You don't have to guilt or shame anyone into getting involved in your ministry, as so many churches do. Instead, people live and breathe it.

Disney's goal is to get guests so immersed in their experience that they forget about the outside world. For instance, when you are on the Jungle Cruise or the Kilimanjaro Safari at Disney's Animal Kingdom, Disney wants you so immersed in the experience that, for a moment, you forget that you're in Florida. When you go on Mission: Space they don't want you to feel like you're going on a space-themed ride, but that you are training to be an astronaut. It's the ability to allow you to suspend reality that Disney does so well. This is what makes the experience "magical" for most folks and why we're willing to repeatedly spend our vacation dollars at the Disney parks. Yes, we all know there's no such thing as a six-foot-tall talking mouse. Yet most adults, upon seeing Mickey Mouse, lose their minds. They're yelling, "It's Mickey!" not, "It's some random guy in a mouse costume!" Whether they have children or not doesn't seem to matter. They get caught up in the magic. Why? Because when you are in the Disney parks you are completely immersed in that environment and it's okay for kids to be kids and it's okay for adults to be kids, too.

This environment goes back to our discussion about intentionally creating your culture. "Church" should not be something we do or a place to which we go. Being a Christ-follower should be who we are. I've heard the phrase "The church is not the building but the people" more times than I can count. Usually it's a nice little colloquialism that has everyone nodding and smiling when they hear it, but it has little to no impact on how we actually "do" church.

Imagineers are able to create such great stories because they live and breathe stories. All of the various books I've read and interviews I've conducted reiterate that Imagineers tell stories constantly, whether in their office or on break. It's just who they are. Whether they were that way before working for Disney is hard to say, but from day one of working at Walt Disney Imagineering (WDI) they are immersed so thoroughly in the culture of storytelling that it becomes who they are, not just what they do.

Can you say the same about your church? Are the ministries what people "do" or does it flow out of who they are? True Blue Sky thinking comes from the core of your being. It's part of your passion. It is not just an idea or copying what someone else has done. If you want to help people move from "doing" to "being," create an environment of immersion in your community of faith. When one becomes involved in the community of faith, one should forget the "other" world. Others should no longer see a separation between that person's "church self," "work self," and "home self." Instead, others begin to see a holistic person—the same no matter where that person is.

Accomplishing this shift in attitude will require a lot of intentional discipleship. Personally, make sure you are at this place. It's hard to lead someone where you aren't going too. Ask your pastor to preach and teach on "being" followers of Christ as opposed to "doing" ministry. Talk in your ministry teams about what you can do to create an immersive ministry environment as opposed to events that people volunteer for or come to. Once you begin to accomplish this environment then the ideas for future ministries and expansion of ministries will flow in a much more organic fashion, rather than trying to copy the latest and greatest fad.

GET REAL!

Once you have your dream, your story, and your immersive ministry environment, move into the Blue Sky process of brainstorming, asking, "what if." From that meeting, begin to cull the many possibilities into several realistic ideas. I mentioned before that there would come a time for your budget and resources to come into play. This is that time. Go down the list of ideas and honestly evaluate each one: definite possibility, not yet, not for us, and no way. At this point you might be thinking, "Chris, you're just telling me the basics of brainstorming. How is this any different?" Good question. I'm glad you asked. The difference between "brainstorming" and "Blue Sky" is that brainstorming still focuses on what you can do. Blue Sky has no limitations. It's an attitude. In action, brainstorming and Blue Sky will look very similar. The difference is in the mindset. Do you see endless possibilities or do you only let your mind wander to what's "realistic"? I've sat in on many church planning sessions where we did a round of brainstorming, but rarely do I see the freedom, innovation, and creativity that is called for in Blue Sky. So, brainstorming = still limited thinking. Blue Sky = unlimited thinking.

Let's look at the categories I listed for evaluation. They are not random. "Definite possibility" should be used for any idea that fits the mission and vision of the church, as well as being within the scope of reality in relation to available resources. "Not yet" should be applied to any idea that fits the mission and vision of the church, but the ingredients necessary for implementation (such as money or human resources) are not currently available. Do not discard these ideas. Every ministry team in your church should have a folder full of "not yet" ideas. They need to be reevaluated on a regular basis. "Not yet" ideas can stay in the folder as long as they fit that category, but you don't want those to collect dust and never see the light of day again. "Not for us" applies to an idea that might be excellent for ministry, but it does not fit within the mission and vision of your community of faith. Most churches cannot be everything to everyone. We all have limited resources, so it is vital that we focus on doing what we do really well. When you look at an idea and think, "That's a great idea, but it's not really who we are as a local community of faith," then ask yourself, "Who does fit this idea?" Since I'm in the Bible Belt I can't throw a rock off the front porch without hitting a church. They are all around me. Surely one of them would fit this idea. So I pass the idea along to that church. Finally, "no way" is an idea that really doesn't belong as a ministry. It wouldn't accomplish anything towards making disciples. Those are often "silly" or off-the-wall ideas that come out of a free and innovative meeting. Discarding them as "no way" does not make them worthless. Those are part of the process and can often be fun. Some of the craziest "no way" ideas lead to the best "definite possibilities."

Once your ideas are sorted it's time to start again. You can put the latter three categories away, but you also need to evaluate your "definite possibilities." You might have five or six definite possibilities in front of you, but only the resources to do one at this moment. This can, potentially, be one of the most difficult parts of the process. A couple of the Disney Imagineers I spoke with described the ideas as being a bit like their children. They have a hard time giving up on any of them, but they also realize that is a necessary part of the process. I'm sure some of the folks on the ministry team will feel the same way. Sometimes the Imagineers scrap all the ideas and start over. Sometimes they combine ideas. Sometimes they pick one and go with it. A good example is the current Fantasyland expansion project going on at the Magic Kingdom. The initial plan was to build a couple of rides, a new "Beauty and the Beast" themed restaurant, some princess meet-and-greet locations, and Pixie Hollow, which would be based around the new Tinkerbelle series. After a good bit of reflection, Tom Staggs, the new chair of Walt Disney Parks and Resorts, decided that the expansion plans were too young girl–focused and wanted to target a wider demographic. So they have modified the plans. Disney's creative culture allows for shifts midstream when they see they aren't hitting their target. Staggs said, "Our process is always iterative and always goes through changes as it goes along. I believe one of my most important jobs is to make sure that I'm enabling and challenging our creative process to create the best possible result."[9]

An important part of the Blue Sky process is not to get too personally attached to any one idea. This is a difficult tightrope to walk. On the one hand, you want the idea to be intricately a part of who you are. On the other hand, you have to be willing to release that idea to the creative process. Once the idea is out there, it is no longer "yours" but "ours." Adopting this attitude will allow the greatest possible conclusion.

How, then, do we decide on which idea out of all of the "definite possibilities" is the best one to pursue? ABC's *Nightline* program aired a feature about the IDEO corporation.[10] IDEO is, essentially, a think-tank that revamps old ideas into creative new ones. In this particular episode, IDEO was given the objective of creating a new style of shopping cart. They have a process that is very similar to the Blue Sky process, which they call the

"Deep Dive." They come up with a wide variety of ideas and then, like us, come to the point of evaluation. In order to best evaluate they go talk to the people this new idea will impact most. In this case they spoke with people who worked in the grocery stores as well as many customers. They showed them some of the prototype ideas and received feedback on how to improve those ideas. After collecting all of this feedback, they were able to make a much better, more informed decision on how to proceed.

If you're going to make ministry ideas work, you're going to need to put in some time doing research. How will you know if your idea is appealing to its intended target if you never speak with the target? In fact, how will you know your assumptions about what the target "needs" are correct if you don't ask the target? You may be working hard to design a new shopping cart when what the store really needs is a way to make the lower shelves more appealing. How will you know the capabilities of your people to implement the idea if you don't speak directly with those will be doing the implementation? The quick answer is "you won't." I have seen countless ideas come out of church meetings and then fall flat on their face simply because we didn't do our homework. Sometimes we found the need we thought we were addressing wasn't really a need at all. Sometimes the people implementing the ministry were woefully unprepared or hadn't fully bought into the vision. If you take the time to talk to your workers and your intended target, you will get a much clearer idea about which of your "possibilities" you should proceed with.

The reason I suggest doing this "market research," for lack of a better term, is that just because an idea is good does not mean you should implement it. Ask, "What benefit will this ministry bring to our community or church?" If you can't specifically name the benefit, toss the idea into one of the other categories. Then talk with your target to make sure the perceived benefit fits a real need. Again, if not, toss it into one of the other categories.

Once you decide on the one idea that you're going to implement, be it selecting one from all of the ideas or combining ideas, then take the remaining ideas and put them into the "not yet" or "not for us" groups. Don't ever throw out a good idea. You never know when God's timing might provide that idea the green light.

When you have your idea firmly in mind but before you actually implement, it's time to follow Disney's concept of "storyboarding" or "previs" (short for previsualization). Before the Imagineers ever start building a new ride or the artists begin drawing the first frame of a new film they flesh out their ideas through a storyboard. You probably won't do a storyboard, but the point of this stage is to flesh out the concepts (that is, the vision) that is in the mind of those dreaming up this idea. It's the first stage in moving towards reality. Storyboards allow you to actually visualize what's going to happen. Through advanced computer modeling, Disney Imagineers can now see potential conflicts with their designs and ride through their ride before one inch of dirt is physically moved.[11] This previsualization saves massive amounts of time and money by dealing with the conflicts before they physically happen.

Storyboard all of your ideas as well. What will this ministry actually look like "with skin on"? How will your target audience perceive the ministry? What resources are needed? What potential conflicts could arise? What will the physical setting for this ministry look like? Will it be inviting to guests? Will the environment create the right atmosphere for what you're trying to achieve? I strongly recommend that you research the concept of storyboarding and apply the principles to your leadership teams because, by thinking through all of these ideas before you ever implement, you will save yourself a lot of frustration in the long run.

PUT IT INTO ACTION

The last part of Walt's motto was "do." The biggest dreams are worthless if they are never put into action. I've have seen churches plan themselves to death. If a football team practices twenty-four hours a day but refuses to play a game, their practice is worthless. So it is with your plans. Yes, some risk is involved, especially when trying to live a life of faith and accomplish a BHAG. You can't eliminate risk, which means there will always be some level of fear involved.

The problem many church leaders run into is that they think they have to eliminate all fear and objections before acting on a plan. Thus a fantastic plan might, to use the political term, never make it out of committee. If you look at a bell curve, at the beginning you have those who will jump on board for any new idea (innovators) and at the end you have those who will never agree no matter how good the idea (never adaptors). Throughout the rest of the curve there are early, middle, and late adaptors. Those on the left and right side of the curve will be frustrated with each other and the middle adaptors will feel caught in the middle. This is, essentially, the way it goes with any new idea, no matter how good your leadership, so just expect it.

There are a couple of ways you can help things go more smoothly, though. Church strategist Charles Arn suggestes, "Introduce the idea as an addition not a replacement, and introduce the idea as a short-term experiment, not a long-term commitment."[12] I have found these two ideas particularly helpful in implementation. Many late and never adaptors fear change. They don't want to lose what they already love about your church. Disney faces this constantly. Since Disney World has now been around forty years, and Disneyland sixty, multiple generations have grown up with these parks. In order for Disney to add something new it sometimes means the removal of something old. Disney faced severe backlash when they removed such classics as Horizons and World of Motion from Epcot to add the new rides Test Track and Mission: Space. Disney took a different tack in 2009 when they unveiled their Fantasyland expansion. They couched it as an addition to the existing Fantasyland as opposed to wiping out the current Fantasyland and starting over. People will usually jump on board with something new if it doesn't threaten what they already love.

The other idea is to propose everything as a short-term experiment. Don't invest 100 percent in any ministry program. You invest in people, not programs; ministry, not buildings. If a program doesn't work, be prepared to say, "We tried. That didn't work. Let's try something else." No big deal. I love the show "Mythbusters" on the Discovery Channel. Adam Savage, one of the hosts, is famous for saying, "Failure is always an option!" Don't be afraid to experiment and fail. If you present something as a long-term commitment, gambling the church's self-esteem and future on the idea, and it fails—you're in big trouble. If, however, you present the same idea as "Let's try it and see what happens," failure becomes seen as part of the learning process, not "failure" as we typically think of it in the negative sense. Jack Gillett, an Imagineer, said, "Nothing should be easy. If you don't fail some of the time, then you're not pushing hard enough. And those failures are usually the best learning tools."[13]

A final concept you must grasp is that you will never win 100 percent approval. A truly innovative and creative idea is always going to be met with some level of resistance. Some people might even leave your church. I don't want you to hear me saying, "Who cares?" It breaks my heart to see people walking out of a church home. However, we must also realize that we can't allow the vision of God to be hijacked by a few. There is an order to things. God's story, the gospel, is the metanarrative. God's story is bigger than the story of any individual church (macronarrative) or individual member (micronarrative). The goal of every church is to figure out how it's vision and story (macronarrative) fits within the overall metanarrative of God. Then, it's up to each individual to connect their individual narrative with the church's story. The micronarrative of the individual can never be considered more important than the macronarrative or the church, and definitely not more than the big story of God. As a leader in the church, help these people to find where they fit, but if they refuse, you can't compromise the overall mission and vision. If the vision God has given your church isn't for those persons, send them on with your blessings. Let them go to a church where they do connect with the vision rather than trying to force-feed them your vision or dropping your vision to make them happy.

Once you're ready to go, set a specific date, to implement the new ministry. In order to set your date you need to outline the exact resources you will need to make the ministry succeed. Have a "drop date" for the ministry in mind. That is, if you don't have all the resources in place by a certain date then you push back the launch. Don't ever launch halfway. I take the NASA approach to launching new ministries. If all systems aren't 100 percent go, we scrub the launch and aim for another day. Better to scrub and wait to be fully ready than to launch unprepared and fail.

Once the resources are in place, make sure also that the timing is right. Marty Sklar instructs the Imagineers, "Avoid overload—tell one story at a time."[14] In other words, don't try to launch three different new ministries at the same time. Get one off the ground before you aim for another. Every new ministry needs your utmost attention during its infancy. If you try to do too many things you'll end up not doing any of them well.

Once you launch, that is not the end of the process. You also need to set up evaluation dates and criteria for evaluation. How will you know if the ministry is a success or failure? Is it the number of lives changed? Money given? People attending? It's up to your implementation team to set the criteria. Use that criteria at regular intervals to determine if the ministry is succeeding or not. You don't want to get six months down the road and realize something's not right. Better to fix it quickly. My suggestion for evaluation is after the first week, then two weeks later, then monthly for the first three months. Once you get to that stage you can determine if you still need to meet monthly or if you want to space your evaluations out more. By that time you should have a good grasp on how well the ministry is doing and any changes that need to be made.

Finally, don't be afraid to stop a ministry if it's not working. Remember: "Failure is always an option." I have spoken with some of the top pastors from around the world, including pastors from the United States, England, Canada, Egypt, Israel, Zimbabwe, Mexico, Brazil, South Korea, and others. Unanimously they all said for every great success that you hear about they have twenty or more failures that you don't. The key is that they have created an environment of innovation where failures are seen as a positive, not a reason to quit. Most great scientists will tell you they have learned more from their experiments that failed than the ones that succeeded. Implement your ministry with that spirit of adventure. If you do, regardless of the "success" of the ministry, you'll never fail.

CONCLUSION

Our theme for this chapter has been "dream big." One of the biggest draws about Disney is its ability to inspire dreams. People so lose themselves in the magic of the experience that they forget that mice can't talk, you can't really go on a mission to Mars, and dinosaurs and yetis aren't everyday sights. To pull off that kind of suspension of reality is pretty impressive.

In your church you aren't trying to get people to suspend reality. Instead, you're trying to get them to suspend disbelief in themselves and in the system. The two things that most often stop people from dreaming big for God is the belief in their own inadequacy and believing the system won't allow them to accomplish anything, so why bother trying. As a church leader you can help change the system so that your church is an environment that encourages creativity and innovation. You can also be a coach to others to encourage them, individually, to rely on God's strength and believe that anything is possible.

I encourage you to start the Blue Sky process with your leadership teams. With God's power behind you, if you all start acting as if the sky is the limit, you'll discover there is no limit for God, and you will accomplish more than even your dreams would have led you to believe.

★

LIVING INTO THE LESSON

1. Do you, personally, approach new opportunities with fear and trepidation or with passion and excitement? How about your church?

2. What is your BHAG (Big, Hairy, Audacious God-goal)—personally and as a church or ministry team?

3. Who are you as a community of faith? Are you constantly trying to keep up with the latest fad? Are you stuck in the past?

4. Who do you want to be as a community of faith?

5. When presented with a new ministry, how do you approach making the decision? Do you ask "what" or "what if"?

6. Are your ministries attached to a story? How has the presence or absence of a story affected your success?

7. Are your ministries simply what you are doing or do they flow out of being followers of Christ? Are your members immersed in the community of faith?

8. How do you currently view failure? Is it part of the learning process or a negative outcome?

9. How can you implement Blue Sky thinking in your church right now? What steps do you need to take first?

FOUR ★ ATTENTION TO DETAIL

If people knew how hard I work to get my mastery,
it wouldn't seem so wonderful after all.

—MICHELANGELO

Part of what makes walking through a Disney park such a magical, immersive experience is the incredible attention to detail. Attention to detail is more than just creative theming, which we have already discussed. Allow me to share with you two of my favorite examples. In the middle of Disney's Animal Kingdom is a huge cell phone tower. Unless you know exactly what to look for, however, I seriously doubt you'll find it. The Imagineers have disguised it as a giant tree. When you are supposed to be walking through the savannahs of Africa or the jungles of Southeast Asia, Disney does not want you to see a giant cell phone tower. That would take you out of the magic and back into reality. It's possible that you would never notice that tower, but Disney takes no chances. They are committed to detail so that your experience stays as transcendent as possible.

Another example comes from Epcot. If you stand near the Mexican pavilion in the World Showcase and look across the World Showcase Lagoon toward Morocco you can clearly see, in the distance, the back of the Twilight Zone Tower of Terror, which is located in Disney's Hollywood

Studios. When the Imagineers realized that guests would be able to see Tower of Terror while in Epcot, they intentionally designed the back of the Tower of Terror to blend in with Morocco. It has turrets and a similar paint scheme so that it doesn't stick out. Many guests probably never notice it, but Disney's attention to detail makes sure that you are never reminded that you're in a theme park. They want you to stay within the "magic" of being in the midst of all of the countries.

Attention to detail is about going the extra mile. Most guests at Walt Disney World don't realize that they are seeing the back of the Tower of Terror. Disney didn't set out to decorate the Tower of Terror because everyone noticed it. Instead, they decorated it the way they did just so that it did not stick out. The Imagineers went out of their way to create something that guests wouldn't notice so that the magic of Epcot wouldn't be ruined. That's way beyond what is "normal" and expected, but going that extra mile is what makes Disney so unique.

Nothing illustrates attention to detail better than the process Disney went through in creating Expedition: Everest, a roller coaster that opened in 2006. The story behind this ride is that the guests are going on an expedition into the Himalayan Mountains in search of the yeti, a mythical "Bigfoot"-like creature. During the ride guests go high into the "mountains" and encounter the yeti, which leads to a thrilling finish to the ride.

Disney Imagineers could have simply used their imagination to create their concept of the yeti, the mountains, and the ride queue. No one would have noticed. After all, Disney is supposed to be about suspending reality. Detail, however, is vital for Disney. The Imagineers sent their design team to Nepal to do an in-depth study of the culture and how people perceived the yeti. They asked locals for detailed descriptions of what the yeti looked like and how the creature is suppose to act. They also took detailed notes on the architecture and traditions of the area. All of this combined to make a truly immersive experience. When you go through the Expedition: Everest queue, you almost believe you've been transported to Nepal because the attention to detail is so great. This ride queue is one in which I would happily wait an hour to ride the ride because the detail of the queue is immersive enough that you find something new every time you go through.

The yeti itself is another example of attention to detail. The Imagineers easily could have created a cartoon-like monster, but they wanted something that looked, acted, and felt like a real animal. The result of all of their research is very impressive. Unfortunately, the yeti is also one of the failures the Imagineers are using as a learning experience. When Expedition: Everest was designed the Imagineers made sure that the mountain, ride track, and yeti were three completely separate structures that did not touch each other at all. This was to reduce wear and the load on the structures. The yeti was the most advanced animatronic ever built. However, it has turned out to have been improperly designed. The stress on the animatronic is so great that Disney can no longer run it as it was intended without fear of the creature ripping itself apart. Thus, as of the fall of 2010, they have had to resort to keeping the monster mostly still and using a strobe-light to simulate motion. In most theme parks the effect of the current yeti would still cause a "wow" factor. However, guests expect so much of Disney that the yeti's inability to run in "A" mode has caused great consternation and chatter on the Disney fan websites. When you raise expectations, you better make sure that you meet those expectations or there will be backlash. I am highly interested to see how the Imagineers handle this issue going forward.

Thus far I've given you some large-scale examples of how Disney's attention to detail helps create the magic. It is often the small details, however, that make you smile the most. My favorite of these small details is at the "Muppet*Vision 3-D" attraction in Disney's Hollywood Studios. As you walk into the attraction, if you will look to your right you will see what looks like an old theater ticket window. There's a sign on it that says "Back in 5 minutes. Key under the mat." If you lift up the mat in front of the window you will, indeed, find the key lying there.

It doesn't matter how many trips to the Disney parks I take, I always discover something new. It doesn't have to be something flashy. Susan Veness says, "Magic flows out of the tricks you don't see. . . . Disney magic is even more elusive. Some say it's in the attractions, some say it's in the atmosphere, and some credit the can-do attitude of the Cast Members. But nearly everyone who visits the parks agrees: The magic is there; they just can't quite put their finger on where. And like the magician, Disney's magic also lies in the sleight of hand, the hidden detail."[1] If you want go get an idea of the breadth of the details Disney puts into their attractions, then pick up Susan's book, *The Hidden Magic of Walt Disney World*. That book contains more than two hundred pages of little details that you can find in the parks. And I'm sure she hasn't covered them all.

Finding the Disney details has attracted an almost cult-like following. There are many websites and several books related to finding "hidden Mickeys." A "hidden Mickey" is the three-circle mouse-head (two circles for ears with a larger circle for the head) that is the famous Disney symbol. The Imagineers plant these "hidden Mickeys" all over the place. One easy example: If you're riding through the Haunted Mansion, examine the table closely in the dinner scene. You will see a place setting set up with the big dinner plate flanked by two smaller plates to form the ears.

While all of this might seem interesting, you might be thinking, "What does this have to do with my church?" Everything. Details are what separate good churches from great churches. We're not in competition with each other. We're all on the same team for God, which means we all need to learn these lessons so that every church can be successful. Attention to detail is important whether you are a large, multistaff church or a little country church that can barely afford a part-time pastor. Your commitment to detail will make a huge difference in your success for God.

When Nick Saban took over as the head football coach for the University of Alabama in 2007, the program was in disarray. Alabama had seen numerous years of up and down seasons. Nick Saban took the team from 7-6 his first year to undefeated National Champions in 2009. Most of the players who started the championship game were recruited by the former coach. How did Coach Saban turn the program around so quickly? A lot of it has to do with his obsession over attention to detail. From the moment he was hired he paid attention to every detail of the program, including practice schedules, work-out schedules, the color paint used in the locker rooms and coaching offices, the stadium, the field conditions, and so on. He considers no detail too small to consider.[2]

If a football coach can be that obsessed with details over something as relatively unimportant as a football game (I realize, living in the state of Alabama that I am speaking blasphemy here), how much more should we care about details? We carry the most important message ever given to humankind. No detail should be beneath our consideration.

Details are important because they help you stay focused on the process of implementing your ministry and they convey to your target audience how important they are. Jimbo Fisher, head coach of Florida State University, was the offensive coordinator for Nick Saban at LSU. He has modeled much of his coaching philosophy after Saban's. He said, "You hear coach Saban talking about it all the time—process-oriented thinking as opposed to outcome-oriented thinking. Sometimes you want to win so fast you don't know how to win." Fisher went on to discuss how vital it is to get the players to buy into every detail of the system. He said he wants to change "How they walk. How they talk. How they breathe." so that they become winners.[3]

I especially appreciate Fisher's comment about wanting to win too quickly. All of us want successful churches. We want to see new people, new ministries, and lives being changed. The problem is that we sometimes become so focused on the results that we forget the details of the process. Becoming a successful church is about every person doing the little things right every single day. If you aren't committed to the process of transformation, you'll never achieve success in your church. And by "you" I am not referring to a generic "you." I mean "you," the person reading this book, not "you" tell others that they need to pay attention to the details. Whether you are a lay leader or a pastor is irrelevant. All of us must be committed to the small details in order to succeed. Continuing the sports analogy, if the quarterback is committed to details but the offensive line isn't, the quarterback is still going to be sacked quite a lot. All of us have to work together.

Achieving a culture where details are important is a process. It won't happen overnight. The leaders must commit to the idea first, and then they must model that attitude for the rest of the church. Disney is obsessive about details because Walt was obsessive about details. Walt then imparted that attitude to his original Imagineers and animators. They, in turn, modeled the attitude for all new employees until it became so ingrained in the corporate culture that now the attitude of attention to detail is part of what Disney is best known for. Even today, though, every Cast

Member has to embrace the idea or it can all fall apart in a heartbeat. It's very frustrating that it can take years to build something into the DNA of your company or church, but it doesn't take long at all for that attitude to fall away. Attention to detail is part of the narrative of what Disney, the brand, is. Does your church carry that same narrative? If not, start telling stories about why attention to detail is important and help those around you to make that connection.

WHAT DETAILS?

You might now ask, "What details should I be concerned about?" The simple answer is: all of them. Nothing is too small. However, let's take some time to examine the types of details that are important for a successful church.

Can you tell me why your children's Sunday school rooms are painted the color that they are? Maybe I should begin with the smaller detail of asking whether you can tell me the color that those rooms are painted. John Hench, an Imagineering legend, insisted on getting the colors for every Disney attraction perfect. Can you imagine if the Haunted Mansion were painted bright yellow? Or what if Cinderella's Castle were bubblegum pink? Color matters. It sets mood and helps convey the story.[4] Perhaps you want to create a calm, contemplative mood. Then consider using a blue color or shade of green. If you want to have a room with lots of energy, use a yellow. If you want to help keep minds free from clutter then consider using a white. The list goes on. My point is that even the colors you use in your facilities should be details that are thought through carefully. Disney is so fanatical about details that every park castle is given a custom paint scheme that will give off an aura of fantasy based on the interplay of sunlight and clouds in that location, whether in Tokyo, Anaheim, Orlando, Paris, or Hong Kong.[5]

If you want to do a thorough, detailed, analysis of your facilities, start on the outside and work your way in. What does your parking set-up say to people? If you have tons of handicapped parking, that's very welcoming to handicapped people. It could also signal to outsiders that your church is "old." Do you have any first-time visitor designated parking? That tells people that visitors are important and that you expect visitors. Do you have expectant mother parking? That tells people you are a young, growing church. How clean and well-maintained is your parking lot? Is there any trash? Are the lines well-painted? Those details in the parking lot say a lot about who your congregation is before someone even walks through the door.

Once you get inside the facilities, I suggest you find a group of people who do not attend your church to do a walkthrough and give you a report. When we walk through our buildings day after day we become blind to many of the details. I do this "mystery shopper" analysis on a regular basis, sometimes during worship and sometimes during the week when no one else is here. I want people to tell me what I'm missing. Recently, one of the "mystery shoppers" showed me a nail sticking out of one of my pews. I had walked right by it without noticing for months. These kinds of issues make it clear to any visitors whether you care or not. You might think, "Why would anyone care about a nail?" Chances are they don't. But if they see it, then it sends a signal about a sloppy, lazy attitude at the church. Have your "mystery shopper" walk through the church and report to you in detail so that you can address these issues without your guests ever noticing.

The greatest details are the ones no one ever notices. Disney does not want you to get on the Twilight Zone Tower of Terror worried about how the ride works. They just want you to enjoy the experience. Engineers, artists, designers, and operators have all worked out the details so that they don't have to be your concern. However, if something went wrong you'd be concerned in a hurry! You'd start wondering about all of the safety back-up mechanisms and how well they work. This is how it should be within your church. People don't need to notice and appreciate every little detail. The fact that you, as a church leader, take care of these details will ensure a better experience for your guests. When you miss one of them, you'll hear about it, but that goes back to the culture of excellence I discussed earlier. When you set high expectations, people will hold you to them.

Details do not have to be anything fancy. Disney is constantly closing various rides for refurbishment. Since the park is open 365 days a year they can't do all of their maintenance at once. When a ride is closed, though, they don't just put up a "closed" sign. Even their "closed" signs are themed.

When the Country Bear Jamboree was closed, the sign read, "The Country Bears need a few days to tune their instruments. We'll be playing again soon." When It's A Small World closed, the sign read, "We're making the 'world' a better place." No one would have complained had the signs read "closed" and nothing else. However, the extra touch of those signs, that little detail, is part of the Disney magic. Attention to detail is going beyond what you "have" to do, whether anyone else notices or not.

Details are not just facility related. Important details are found in every aspect of church life. How do you handle first-time visitors? Do you have an intentional process for moving people from guests to attendees to active members? Do all of your leaders know what to do in the event of an emergency? Who monitors the weather if the threat of severe weather occurs during a time the building is in use? How are prayer needs spread through the church?

I do a lot of disaster response training for the United Methodist Committee on Relief (UMCOR). Part of that training is teaching churches and disaster response teams that the worst-case scenario is the one you can't think up. You have to try to be ready for most every contingency, and part of that readiness is adopting the attitude that no details are too small. I ask questions about church records: What would happen to your church records if the church burned? Do you keep backups offsite? Who knows where the records are kept and how to access the backups? How would your church handle a local disaster? What if your church building were hit by a tornado—where would you worship and how would you function? What if a flu pandemic hits your area—how would you continue to minister to your people if you can't physically gather together? These are the kind of detail-oriented questions that you need to be asking. If you don't ask the difficult questions now, you'll be left floundering when/if those situations arise.[6]

DETAILS CREATE THE ENVIRONMENT

Paying attention to small details will help determine the environment of your church. The stories you tell will convey what's important to you and who is included in your concept of the body of Christ. Using words and symbols intentionally, or intentionally not using certain words and symbols, can convey infinite meaning to those in your community and church family.

One of my favorite Disney examples is the Haunted Mansion. It is chock full of little details that demonstrate the amount of excessive thought that went into its planning. For instance, though the Ghost Host says that there are spirits from all over the world, in reality you will only see European, Mediterranean, and North American ghosts. No "spirits" are currently seen from Asia, Africa (except one Egyptian lady), or South America. Why? The cosmology (the way that culture views the makeup of the universe, including the spiritual world) of these other cultures is very different from the European model. All cultures have a concept of ghosts, but the idea of ghosts carry very different connotations in other parts of the world. This is why the Hong Kong Disneyland doesn't have a version of the Haunted Mansion like the other Disney parks.

Another specific detail from the Haunted Mansion is that there are no child ghosts. Because the Imagineers do not do anything without a reason, you must assume this is intentional. Why would children be left out of the Haunted Mansion when Disney is so focused on children? The Haunted Mansion is supposed to be a light-hearted wink at human fears about death. There are many jokes about death throughout the ride, including the concept of the killer bride in the attic. However, the Imagineers believe (and I agree) that the death of a child is never funny, no matter how you spin it. They intentionally left children out of the Haunted Mansion because they did not, in any way, shape, or form, want to convey the idea that they found the death of a child humorous.

A final detail, which has been pointed out to me by several curious people, is the obvious lack of Christian symbolism throughout the Haunted Mansion. If you go into any cemetery in the Deep South, where the Mansion is set, you will see an overwhelming amount of Christian symbolism on the tombstones and mausoleums, yet not one cross or religious symbol is seen on any headstone or crypt in the Haunted Mansion. For a group that prides itself on authenticity and details this seems a tremendous oversight! Disney does not have a bias against Christianity, or any religion. They intentionally left religious symbolism out of the attraction. Why? The ride is supposed to be poking fun at death and the

Imagineers did not want people of any religion to get the idea that their faith was being mocked.[7]

These three intentional decisions help make the Haunted Mansion so much fun. No one has to worry about a sudden encounter with something offensive or that would trigger bad memories, such as the death of a child. The Imagineers tried to be respectful and genuine to each culture that was going to be featured in the Haunted Mansion. They are telling a story using a Euro-American mythos, so it doesn't make sense to use other cultures. They are not trying to be exclusive. The Haunted Mansion helps us to laugh at a subject that is generally seen as pretty grim. Only perfect attention to detail allows this to be pulled off so flawlessly.

The Haunted Mansion example has a perfect parallel to the church. Don't try to start a ministry unless it is genuine to the culture around you. Just because something works in California does not mean I should attempt the same ministry in Alabama. I seriously doubt that a surfing ministry would be very successful in my culture.

Also, be aware of the taboos of the culture around you. This is for two reasons. First, you don't want to step on any cultural landmines. Doing something that violates your church or community's culture will be the quickest way to ensure that your ministry does not succeed. Second, you might want to intentionally address those taboos. Maybe you know the community around you has a problem with alcohol or divorce or any other issue that gets swept under the carpet. We want that to be our "dirty little secret." It's the church's prophetic responsibility to address those issues head on. By being aware of the taboos, you can both avoid being offensive as well as speak out when issues need to be addressed.

My doctoral dissertation involved the narratives surrounding divorce and remarriage. I asked several pastors for their views on divorce and remarriage and then I interviewed their congregation members looking for points of congruency, or lack thereof. What I discovered was a serious disconnect between the message the pastors thought they were sending and the message actually being received by those sitting in the pews. The chief reason for this disconnect was a lack of intentionality by the pastors. They assumed their message was getting across without paying attention to the details to make sure that the message wasn't missed.[8]

My research shows just one example of how paying attention to the narratives of your church will impact the ministry. In your ministry team, and in the church as a whole, you can't assume anything. Be intentional about spreading the word about who is included, the message you want the church and community to receive, and the goals you want to achieve. This intentionality is accomplished, largely, by attention to details.

DETAIL ORIENTED, NOT TYRANNICAL

Just because you are detail focused, you do not have the right to become a detail-tyrant. Some folks might take this encouragement to be obsessed with details as a free invitation to become a control freak. That is not what we're after. Control freaks do not function well in the Disney-style church. If you read the myriad of Disney leadership books, you'll see that Imagineers are detail freaks, but not control freaks.

The way to keep individuals from becoming hyper-controlling about the details within the church is to build a culture of discipline. This is, as I mentioned earlier, where every person within the church is equally committed to this culture of attention to detail. Now, I realize it may be a little idealized to say that all are equally committed, but I don't think it's idealistic at all to say that everyone lives out the culture of commitment. If the overarching narrative of your church family is that you care about the little things, and everyone embraces that story, then you won't have to worry too much about control freaks. The family working together will keep any single individual from getting out of control.

Jim Collins, in *Good to Great*, studied many different corporations looking for those measurable factors that helped one company find greatness while another stayed at "good." He writes, "Whereas the good-to-great companies had Level 5 leaders who built an enduring culture of discipline, the unsustained comparisons had Level 4 leaders who personally disciplined the organization through sheer force."[9] To understand what Collins is getting at here you need to understand the difference between a Level 5 and a Level 4 leader. Collins defines a Level 4 leader as a "genius with a thousand helpers" where a Level 5 leader is a leader who builds a superior leadership team around him or her and then together they figure out the path to greatness. A Level 4 leader sets the vision, develops the road map, and then enlists "helpers" who will make his or her vision happen. Level 4 leaders are very good, but they aren't great. Level 5 leaders are great.[10]

Most good churches function with a Level 4 pastor. The pastor sets the vision, develops the path to achieve the vision, and then enlists lay leaders to accomplish the vision. The problem is that as soon as that pastor leaves the entire church falls apart. Dr. Dale Galloway, the dean of my doctoral program at Asbury Theological Seminary, told my class that if the church doesn't last outside of us then we, as pastors and leaders, were failures, regardless of what the church accomplishes while we're there.

This brings us back to Collins's quote. You don't want a situation where attention to detail happens because of the control and focus of one person, whether that person be the pastor or a lay leader. A great church is one in which a culture of discipline exists; where everyone is equally on board with the vision. You want to create a culture within your church where all the people take pride in the little details. I frequently see Disney executives cross the street to pick up a piece of trash. It's part of the corporate culture. Bob Iger even has "picking up trash" in his job description.[11]

Walt Disney constantly asked the question, "How can we do better?" As he asked it more and more, those around him did the same thing. This is the culture you want within your church. Whether we're talking about the worship team, the choir, the trustees, Sunday school teachers, or any other area of the church, we want everyone to ask the same question: "How can we do better?" Unless we ask this question constantly we will slip into complacency. Complacency is one of the worst enemies of excellence and we want to do everything excellently for God. When we become complacent we no longer care about the details. Little things go unnoticed, and before we know it we're in a dying church with run-down facilities. That last statement may seem a little extreme, but the road to irrelevancy in a church is a very slippery slope and it usually begins with complacency.

A perfect example of Disney wanting to avoid complacency is shown when the carousel at Walt Disney World was found to be two inches off center when it was first built.[12] Two inches! Disney moved the carousel because they wanted to make sure that the pictures guests took were perfect. There are many things within your church that might be of similar scale to the "two-inch" problem of the carousel. Do you say, "So what?" or are you committed enough to the small things to do something about it? Your answer to that question will go a long way toward answering how successful you will be in your leadership.

You might initially think that Walt Disney wasted a lot of money on "details." Walt was never a wasteful spender, but he always expected that whatever money was spent on the little details would be returned in guest satisfaction and Cast Member loyalty. Such attention to detail engenders pride among the Cast Members. They are well aware of the tradition of detail at the Disney parks and gain a lot of satisfaction from upholding that tradition.

No church that I've ever encountered has unlimited resources. You can't be frivolous with the money you have, but you also cannot allow someone to control your budget to the point where you won't spend anything. The church is not a corporation, but we are in the business of creating an environment that is conducive to people encountering God. The details matter. The lighting, music, painting, quality of nursery, sound levels, and so on can all make a difference in a person's ability to connect to God. Don't become overly controlling with these details, but give them your full attention.

RESULTS MATTER

Paying attention to detail also means you pay attention to results. This does not mean you are results-oriented. As I mentioned earlier, the process is the most important aspect—moving people from where they are to a closer place in their relationship with God. However, results are not unimportant. Paying attention to the details of results will show you where you are successful and where you need to give more effort.

No one, in my opinion, combines the results/process orientation better than Benjamin Zander, conductor of the Boston Philharmonic. On the first day of class in each semester at the New England Conservatory, Ben informs his new students that they have already achieved an A for the course. The caveat is that within the first two weeks of class the students must submit an essay, dated at the end of the semester, which begins with the words, "Dear Mr. Zander, I got my A because . . ." Ben prohibits using words such as "I hope," "I guess," or "I imagine" from these essays. He wants the students to write as if in retrospect, outlining all of their insights and accomplishments gained during the year ahead. He then encourages the students to live up to their essays. The grades at the end of the semesters are based on whether the students lived up to their goals.[13]

Ben forces the students to imagine their future in great detail. He doesn't allow generalities or wishes. This process is a great way for churches to approach results. You don't want those on your ministry team obsessed over how many people show up or how much money is given. Sometimes those things are out of your control. If you live in a place with a declining population, seeing numerous new faces walk through your door might not be realistic, but there are other ways to measure the results of your ministry.

If you are a ministry team leader, tell everyone on your team, using Zander's concept, "This ministry has already earned an A for the evaluation we're going to do in x months." That frees everyone from performance anxiety. But then ask, "Why do we deserve an A?" Coax the details out of your team members. Don't let them settle for "we tried hard." Let them raise the standard and then publish those standards and encourage them to live up to their dreams. When it comes time to evaluate ministry, all you have to ask is, "Did we live up to our A?"

This is not to say that people and budgets are totally unimportant. I've heard some pastors, trying to sound holy, inform me that they "don't care about numbers." For me, though, every number represents a human being whom Christ loves and gave his life to save. Every dollar that comes in is more ministry that we can accomplish. When viewed through those lenses, numbers become pretty important. They shouldn't be your sole criteria, but neither should they be dismissed.

We talked in chapter 1 about "Bump the Lamp." That means doing the right things the right way down to the tiniest detail. Is your church ready to make that commitment? Are you ready to get fanatical about details so that lives can be transformed?

CONCLUSION

Not every person is a detail person. Some people are naturally obsessed with details while others become frustrated and bogged down by details. That's okay. God made us different and we celebrate that uniqueness. Every successful leader, however, needs to care about the details. If you are a "big picture" type of person, make sure you have people on your ministry team who are good at managing the details. This does not mean that you can excuse yourself from the details. If you're going to be a successful leader then you need to stay on top of the details, even if you allow others on your team to handle them.

Like Walt, your ministry team should constantly be asking, "How can we do this better?" Most often the "better" is found in the details. Once the big picture concept is in place, there is not much you can do to improve it. The vision may shift slightly over time as you respond to the specific needs of those around you, but it is in the details where you can really make improvements.

The frustrating part, for some, about details is that you may not get a lot of pats on the back for all of your hard work. The details make so much difference in the effectiveness of a ministry and yet it continues to amaze me how many people in the pews never notice those details. They notice when something is missed or goes wrong, but they generally never notice when everything is flowing smoothly. They'll notice "something" is different about your church compared to others, but they may not be able to put their finger on it. That's okay. It's important for you to accept the reality that details do not often bring personal glory, but we minister for God's glory, not our own, anyway. Details do, however, make a big different in the impact on others.

I very much enjoyed visiting the Vineyard Community Church in Cincinnati, Ohio. They are known for servant evangelism.[14] Their motto, which is carved into their building where people are reminded constantly, is, "Small things done with great love will change the world." That is the attitude of details. Paying attention to all of the small things is an act of love. That's why it makes a difference. It shows those you are serving just how much you care. Almost anyone can dream up the "big picture" for a ministry, but when you care enough about others to invest in the details, you will see lives changed.

★

LIVING INTO THE LESSON

1. Think about an example where attention to detail has made a difference for you, personally.

2. Where have you seen attention to detail make a difference in your church? Or have you?

3. How is your church or ministry committed to details?

4. Where do you need closer attention to details?

5. What do the details in your church or ministry (or personal life) say about you?

6. What steps do you need to take to give the attention to detail you desire? What needs attention first?

7. Do you have a designated person or group to handle the details? How will you engage everyone in the attention to detail?

8. How committed are you to getting the details right? How can you improve upon that?

9. Imagine and discuss in detail how you want your church or ministry to look. How will you begin to achieve that dream?

FIVE ★ TRAINING

Success in training the boy depends largely
on the Scoutmaster's own personal example.

—ROBERT BADEN-POWELL,
founder of the Boy Scout movement

For the last few years I have practiced "muso jikiden eishin-ryu," a Japanese samurai sword marital art that traces its beginnings back several hundred years. During a seminar, Carl Long, a sensei from Pennsylvania and one of the leading sword experts in the United States, gave a lecture differentiating the concepts of "jitsu" and "do" (pronounced "doe" like a female deer).[1] You may have heard of jujitsu and judo and wondered about the difference. Martial artists have long debated which is better. In Sensei Long 's explanation, "jitsu" is learning the style. It is gaining mastery over the techniques and polishing them. "Do," on the other hand, is when you have mastered the techniques to such a high degree that you no longer have to consciously think about them to perform them. Your body and mind react together naturally, instinctively.

If you want to understand the current culture of your church family, ask yourself, "What is their 'do'?" What do they do instinctively? If you don't like what you see, then you have to go through a period of training, "jitsu," to change their "do." Training, by definition, means they have not perfected the concepts. There will be mistakes and failures. Once the hard work has been put in, the new way of being will eventually begin to happen naturally. When I first picked up a sword I felt clumsy and awkward. I was constantly frustrated, feeling like I would never be able to move it as gracefully as my classmates. Now I can move it fluently with only a little thought. With more training it will become a natural extension of my body.

To achieve this in the Disney Corporation, every Cast Member must go through Traditions, which is an intensive, total immersion into the Disney culture. I suppose you might even call it "brainwashing," but not in a negative way. The goal is that by the time the new Cast Members complete Traditions they are so immersed in Disney's culture that they react instinctively to fulfill the Disney mission. This is the goal of every type of training.

The purpose of Traditions, originally, was to instill in every Cast Member the concept of the number one job: "We create happiness." This was how Dick Nunis and Van France stated the entire mission when they began the training program for Disneyland Cast Members in 1955. Since 1955, the mission statement has grown a little. It's now, "We create happiness by providing the finest entertainment to people of all ages everywhere."[2] That sounds very nice and corporate, but what will most people remember? "We create happiness." Traditions ingrains that concept into every new Cast Member.

"We create happiness" in action means that Cast Members don't have to seek managerial approval before giving a guest a magical experience. If a Cast Member sees an opportunity to enrich a guest's experience, he or she has full authority to act upon that opportunity. I once saw a little girl crying on Main Street. Her father was explaining to her that they had used up their spending money and couldn't get her a balloon. The little girl wasn't being rude or throwing a temper tantrum. She had wanted a balloon but, as kids often do at Disney World, had used up her allowance too quickly. A Cast Member, apparently overhearing the conversation, came up behind the little girl with a balloon, gave it to her, and said, "Mickey wants you to have this." Then it was the dad whose eyes were filled with tears as the little girl hugged the Cast Member. Do you think that Cast Member understood "We create happiness"?

The interaction with the balloon was not random. Cast Members are trained to make such experiences happen. Disney even has a name for them: Take 5s. The reason for the name is to blow the guest's mind with something magical in less than five minutes. Cast Members are not just trained to look for these opportunities, they are actually held accountable for making them happen.[3] Do you hold those on your ministry team accountable for helping create moments that connect people to God?

This same kind of service is seen in other places. Countless times I have seen a Cast Member, whether a street sweeper, a cashier, or a manager strolling through the park, take a picture for a guest rather than allow Dad to take the picture without him in it. They don't wait to be asked. They approach the guests and offer to take the pictures, which generally results in big smiles from the family. If Disney were not so intentional in their training, some Cast Members might still exhibit the same degree of friendliness and helpfulness. Most, however, probably would not—not because they aren't perfectly wonderful people. It's a matter of knowing what your job is. If you think you'll get in trouble for leaving your post or giving away a balloon you won't do it. However, if you are not only encouraged, but actively trained, to look for those opportunities, then you will look for them often. This is what Traditions does for the Disney culture.

I asked several Cast Members why they felt Traditions is so important, beyond learning their jobs. To summarize their response, in spite of the fact that working at Walt Disney World is seen as a dream job for many people, it can actually be quite stressful. You have to deal with people who are not always so polite or patient while trying to help each person, the rude ones included, to have a magical experience. Sometimes being a Cast Member is relaxing and magical, but there are times when it can be overwhelming and stressful. During those stressful times, you don't need to be thinking, "What should I do?" Often you don't have time. The training helps the Cast Members do their job without worry or hesitation.

Perhaps the greatest example of effective training comes from the military. There is no way to completely simulate the stress of a combat environment, but all armed forces regularly train in as realistic conditions as possible. When the bullets start flying, the stress is unimaginable for someone who has never experienced that situation. Without training, many of the soldiers would freeze up or run away. No clearer example exists than the Battle of Bull Run (also known as First Manassas) in the American Civil War. Young, inexperienced soldiers were given weapons and a uniform and thrown into the battle with no training. When their comrades began dying around them many just lay down on the field, frozen. Others dropped their weapons and ran. It's the natural flight instinct found in every person. The only way to overcome that instinct and ensure that the soldiers are capable of doing their job is through intensive, repetitive training.

The military example is an extreme one. Most people will never know the stress of trying to operate in an environment with other people intent on killing you. I'll give some church-specific examples in the section of this chapter devoted to safety. The lesson from this extreme example, however, translates to any situation. If you want people to act and react certain ways under stress then you must given them intense, and repetitive, training. In the church we try to follow Christ. We want to act the way Jesus acts. Unfortunately, due to a little thing called sin, acting like Jesus is often not the natural reaction for us. When stress comes, when someone upsets us, when things don't go our way, we are sorely tempted to react out of our "human" side. In doing so, we can end up saying hurtful and negative things that we later regret. I cannot count the number of times I have had to spend an hour or more with someone trying to calm hurt feeling caused by another church member's unthinking remarks. We need to train our folks to react properly in various situations.

Other than our team members not knowing how to react and respond properly, the number one complaint I hear from church leaders is lack of training. Many team leaders and committee members within the church have lamented to me at conferences and training events that they feel like they are nothing more than a name on the page. In the United Methodist Church, we have to fill certain positions each year. The temptation, as I've mentioned previously, is to find any warm body who is willing to take that position. Once the position is filled, many pastors and church leaders forget about the position until next year. They seem to assume that the new team members will learn what to do via osmosis. If you want your team to be effective, you must train. This is true whether you are responsible for one area of ministry or many. And it is not just the pastor's job to do the training. Lay leaders are just as capable. If you need help, ask your pastor, but you may be more qualified in the area than he or she is. No matter who does the training, make sure it's done effectively and thoroughly.

Training needs to be done for everyone who might potentially need it in a situation. Cross-training is great. The more people who know the plan, the more likely it is to be enacted. The more people who participate, the more effective your response will be, whether it is reacting to a crisis situation or simply carrying out the mission of the church.

SAFETY FIRST

Let's start with the most extreme, but important, aspect of training: safety. In chapter 1 we discussed creating a culture of safety, but now we need to discuss training to respond to events that do happen. I mentioned previously about how quickly Disney security and Cast Members respond when a crisis-type event occurs. They are able to quickly respond not only because of the culture of safety, but because of very specific training.

Imagine being at a vacation planning resort with well over fifty thousand guests on your property. You see out in the Atlantic Ocean a hurricane coming right for you. You are responsible for the lives of all of these people, not to mention the property of your resort. What do you do?

In 2004, this scenario played out not once, but four times at Walt Disney World. On each occasion Disney World was able to reopen the next day with no loss of life and only minimal property damage. Lee Cockerell, former vice president of operations at Walt Disney World, writes, in regard to 2004's Hurricane Charlie, "When an organization can perform that well in a crisis, it's because its employees have been thoroughly trained. Every single Cast Member at Walt Disney World had rehearsed the emergency preparedness plan many times, and all of them played their roles to perfection. That rigorous preparation not only saved lives and property, but paid off financially. We opened for business the morning after the deluge, and we didn't even meet the deductible on the insurance policy."[4]

Managing more than fifty thousand guests, plus employees and facilities, is not something any church is likely to encounter. The principles, though, are the same. Crises will come. It's not "if" but "when." I wish I could tell you what the crisis will be, but, unfortunately, I am not possessed of that ability. I can't do that for my own church, much less yours. This means we have to prepare for as many eventualities as we can imagine. In my many years as a pastor I've never met anyone who said, "I sure wish we were less prepared." There is no such thing as overtraining.

It's sad to say, but we live in a world of active shooters. Do you know what your church would do if someone broke into the sanctuary in the middle of worship with a gun, other than panic? I wish I didn't have to ask that question about a church, but that very scenario has occurred multiple times in recent years, in both large and small churches. I have a couple of men in my congregation with police training who are armed during any church event. We have discussed, planned, and rehearsed exactly how we would handle such an event. I hope we never have to put that plan into action, but we're prepared in case we do.

On March 27, 1994, I was a meteorology student at Mississippi State University and an intern at the ABC affiliate in Birmingham, Alabama. I witnessed one of the most tragic scenes of my life that day when a F4 tornado made a direct hit on Goshen United Methodist Church, near Piedmont, Alabama, right in the middle of the Palm Sunday worship service. Twenty people, including the pastor's four-year-old daughter and five other children, were killed and more than ninety were injured. They never heard the warning. The official report by Tim Marshall of NOAA stated that an interior hallway of the church building would have provided adequate shelter for the entire congregation had they moved there in time.[5]

Does your church have a severe weather plan? Do you have someone who monitors the weather radio on a Sunday morning if severe weather is threatening? Do you have an accessible NOAA weather radio on at all times? Do you know how you would get your congregation to shelter if there was a need? Has your church trained ushers and other key leaders in this plan and how to implement it? Have you practiced the plan? These questions may seem redundant, but asking them could save lives. Severe weather is the first threat that comes to my mind because of the area in which I live, but you know the threats best for your area. Maybe it's flash flooding or earthquakes. We all need to be prepared for fire.

Any time you have a large gathering of people, a large-scale crisis, such as a severe weather warning, threatens to create a disaster within a disaster. If people panic, more people could be injured just from the actions of those around them. Only a planned response enacted by trained, calm leaders will keep everyone as safe as possible.

Another issue that churches seldom seem prepared to handle are health crises. What if someone becomes ill during Sunday school or a worship service? I have been in the pulpit on three or four occasions when someone in the congregation has passed out. I have also been sitting in the congregation when a similar event has happened. If something like this happens, let me give you a word of advice: the show does not have to go on. The couple of times I've been in the congregation during one of these events I saw the pastor looking like a deer in the headlights. Both times the pastor tried to continue on with the service as if nothing was happening when clearly everyone else was distracted. While I realize we don't want to embarrass the person who has fallen ill, acting "normal" does no good for anyone. As Christians, our number one job is to show love, concern, and compassion for others. Stop the service, and let people have a time of prayer for the person who is ill. Once the person is okay or has been removed from the sanctuary to a more private place, the service can continue if it's appropriate. It's not the end of the world if the pastor doesn't finish his or her sermon. The most critical thing in this type of situation is to let your church family show love to one of their own.

When such an event occurs during your worship service, do you know what to do? Who calls 911? Does your church have an emergency defibrillator? If so, where is it and who has access to it? Do you have multiple people who are trained to use it?

Are all of your nursery workers trained in infant and child first aid? Do they have contact numbers for the parents? Do they have a way of getting in touch with the parents during worship if there is an issue with a child? Do you have a policy on how to respond if a child is reported missing or lost while at church? Are all of your nursery and Sunday school workers trained in signing kids in and out to make sure only parents or a designated adult picks them up?

I haven't listed in these pages every emergency that could occur within your church, but I hope you can take these principles and run with them. Figuring out all of the myriad possibilities for crises in your church is a job for those detail-oriented people I spoke of in the last chapter. Allow them to brainstorm or, if you are one of them, join in the brainstorming, and once the possibilities are on the table, together create a plan and train those around you how to implement that plan.

WHO TRAINS?

Who should be responsible for the training in your church? The pastor? The team leaders? Someone specialized? The answer is "Yes!" Every leader in your church is a trainer. Training is both formal and informal, and both are equally important. When you design your training processes make sure that you intentionally hold your leaders accountable for both types of training.

Formal training is like Disney's Traditions. It is the process by which you learn all of the basics. Every church should have two versions of Traditions. One is a membership class, which spells out clearly for all persons wishing to join the church what is expected of them. Rick Warren, pastor of Saddleback Community Church, commented that if your membership is larger than your attendance then membership doesn't mean much in your church.[6] I agree. Most churches have some sort of membership vows. In the United Methodist Church we ask people to promise to support the church with their prayers, presence, gifts, service, and witness. However, we don't enforce that promise. People come up at the end of the service, are asked the questions, and if they say yes then they are a member. We don't take the time to explain the expectations behind those commitments.

Don't get upset with people for not becoming involved in a ministry or not giving to the church if you don't intentionally train them in that expectation. The first version of Traditions should teach the traditions of your specific church, the ministry opportunities available, the resources available, and how each new member can plug in to those opportunities. Make it a requirement for any potential member to understand these commitments before signing up.

A second version of Traditions should be held for all of those coming on to a new ministry team. In this training you would teach all of your new leaders what the purpose of their team is, what the expectations are as members/leaders, and the basics of how to fulfill that role. If your leadership calendar runs from January to January then I suggest you hold the training for new leaders in November so that they are ready to go on January 1. I try to have the new leadership for the upcoming year selected by October at the latest so that the incoming leaders can be mentored by the outgoing leadership.

And this brings us to the second type of training—informal. The leadership at Disney is constantly encouraged to be on the lookout for the next generation of leaders. If they see a Cast Member who has leadership potential, that Cast Member is provided further training and resources to attempt to develop that potential. Disney does not always go out and post a "management wanted" advertisement. They look at the loyal Cast Members around them and groom them into leaders.

This "homegrown" style of leadership development is often the most effective. Yes, I can go find someone with gifts and talents to lead a ministry team, but the leadership will be so much more effective if I find someone already on the ministry team to mentor into a leadership role. If Disney looks outside of the company for a new leader, then Disney has to invest time and resources teaching that new leader the entire corporate culture. If, on the other hand, they groom an existing Cast Member for a leadership role, that Cast Member is already familiar with the Disney way of doing things. That are already immersed in the culture, which makes their transition to leadership that much more seamless.

The same principle applies to your ministry teams. If you are heading up a ministry team, don't always look on the outside for the next leader. Find the diamond in the rough already on your team. The reason more leaders don't follow this style of leadership development is that, initially, it is more difficult.

The easy way to gain leadership is to hire/select people who already have all the skills and knowledge. No effort is, seemingly, required on your part. Just hand them the keys and let them take off. However, if they are not immersed in the vision and culture that you have so carefully and intentionally tried to create (remember chapter 1?), they might take off on their own path. So, while it seems easier to bring on a "ready-made" leader, in the long run you have to invest just as much, or more, energy in getting the new person ingrained in your culture as you would raising up a leader from within your ranks.

Growing leaders from within means that every person in a leadership position within your church should constantly be looking for his or her replacement. The formal style of training is wonderful, and needed. However, the informal style of training is just as important because it is constant and results in personal and spiritual growth, as well as competency in the ministry you are undertaking. Formal training, generally, results only in an increase in knowledge of skills.

In years past, teachers were the "experts." They were the possessors and dispensers of knowledge and were needed to formally pass along that knowledge to the next generation. The only way a person had access to knowledge was through the expert. This is no longer the case. Thanks to the Internet and the "information age," information on pretty much anything can be gained with a few clicks of a mouse. We live in an age of information overload.

I teach basic religion classes at Huntingdon College in Montgomery, Alabama. To be perfectly honest, there is almost nothing I tell these students in the lectures that they couldn't find out on their own if they were willing to do the research. I am no longer needed as a dispenser of knowledge. However, though we have more information than we can possibly absorb, few know what to do with the information they have. My role needs to shift more from expert to coach.

A coach is one who takes a person where they are and develops them. If they have no skills, then you teach them basic skills. If they have some skills, you take them to the next level. I coach my five-year-old's soccer team very differently than I do my ten-year-old's football team, but I function as a coach in both cases. You will have some new people on your ministry team who need to be taught the basic skills. But training does not stop with the basic skills. Once someone has the basic skills learned, coaching begins.

My sword instructor has told me repeatedly that "black belt" is just the beginning. All earning a black belt means is that you've mastered the basics and are now ready to begin learning fine points. In football, most college, and especially professional, players have the basics mastered. Where coaches make a difference is in teaching the finer points. In this manner, training never stops. If you want to be a good leader, you need to be intentionally training those over whom you have influence at every opportunity.

CREATE "MAGICAL MOMENTS"

While visiting Disney's Animal Kingdom on a recent trip, my wife and sons approached the Kilimanjaro Safari ride. My boys, especially, love this ride and would stay on it almost all day long. A Cast Member struck up a conversation with them at the entrance to the ride. After a couple of minutes he asked them to go with him. He walked them past the lines and up to a separate loading dock. He then told them they were going to get a private safari. They were driven around at a slower speed, which enabled them to take some incredible pictures. No one else was on the vehicle so the Cast Member driving was able to answer questions and point out a lot of neat things my family had never noticed before. When Renae and the boys got off the ride, they called me right away. To this day, all three of them proclaim that experience as one of the most magical of their lives.

This was not a random, chance encounter. It is what Disney terms "Magical Moments." Take 5s, which I mentioned earlier, are spontaneous. Cast Members are trained to look for opportunities, but those opportunities aren't planned in advance. Magical Moments are intentional. The Cast Member that approached my family had been instructed to find a family that looked like they needed a Magical Moment and provide them with the private safari.

Disney plans several of these Magical Moments throughout each day. The Magic Kingdom has a special opening ceremony each morning and one lucky family is chosen to ride in the train with Mickey and his pals to help officially open the Magic Kingdom. Cast Members pick kids out of the crowds during parades to dance. The Festival of the Lion King brings kids on stage for the finale to dance with the characters. The Indiana Jones Stunt Spectacular and the Lights, Motor, Action Stunt Show both have guest families start the show. These are planned experiences that cost Disney no money, yet the guests go home raving about each of these moments. Lee Cockerell writes, in referencing the Take 5s and Magical Moments, "All those seconds and minutes repeated thousands of times a day add up to better customer relations than you could buy with a big corporate PR budget."[7]

Are the leaders in your church trained to create Magical Moments? I get that you're not going to bring up a "guest family" to kick off worship. What I'm talking about is do you have intentional measures in place to make people feel special? Are your leaders being trained to constantly be on the lookout for spontaneous moments where they can really brighten someone's day? Your church can spend as much money as you want on advertising, but it is the way people are treated that will bring them back. People are desperately looking for love in today's culture and, as singer Johnny Lee stated, most of them are "looking for love in all the wrong places." You can profoundly impact lives through simple acts of kindness that cost the church little to no money. As a ministry team, come up with specific, intentional ways to make people feel special, and then also train all of your leaders to look for spontaneous moments to impact someone's life. If you implement this in your church, you'll never need to worry about an advertising budget.

GIVE CONSTANT FEEDBACK

One of the great mistakes many churches make is to train and deploy leaders and then forget about them. As a pastor, I'm required to sit down at least once a year with my Staff-Parish Relations Committee to review my performance, set goals for the next year, and discuss any obstacles that might hinder the achievement of those goals. Sometimes we meet more than once a year. These meetings are helpful, because I'm provided with useful feedback and have the opportunity to share concerns and needs.

How often are the same opportunities provided for you as a church leader? Do you feel like you're trained and then left on your own? Are your rewarded for a good job or given direction when you feel like you're floundering? Do you feel like you can go to whoever supervises your ministry and ask for feedback? Do you intentionally give feedback to those you supervise?

Disney has made a habit of releasing general company-wide statements to all of the Cast Members that tell where things are going well and where they need to step up a little more. Managers are trained to hold regular one-on-one meetings with those they supervise. Disney uses every means possible to let their Cast Members know where they stand, both in terms of excellence and the need for improvement.

The Disney managers are also trained not to just tell people what to do, but to actually explain to those they supervise why various policies and procedures are necessary. Ingrained in every one is that two-year-old child that asks, "Why?" for everything we're told. We do better when we're told why something needs to be done. I help coach my oldest son's football team. When I'm trying to help a ten- or eleven-year-old child understand the need to move in a certain way, it helps to say, "If you lead with your head like this (demonstrate), you're running a big risk of injury. If, instead, you move your hands here (demonstrate) you will see a better result and not get hurt." That works much better than me saying, "For the fiftieth time put your hands here!" Whether we're talking about children or adults, an understanding of "why" will almost always lead to better actions in the future.

STAY PROCESS-ORIENTED

Disney does not send Cast Members through Traditions and then view that as the end of their training. Once Cast Member complete Traditions, they proceed to on-the-job training. After two or three months, they are given another round of training that covers their work area in even more detail. Once new Cast Members have mastered that round of training and feel completely comfortable with their jobs, then they are ready to begin creating those Magical Moments and learning to exceed guest expectations.

Disney does not view their training procedures as an employee factory where they stick a newly hired employee in one end, run him or her through a machine, and out pops a trained Cast Member on the other side. Disney takes a process-oriented approach to training. They realize that a Cast Member can't absorb the entirety of Disney culture by the end of Traditions. It takes time, so they allow for that process to take place. The new Cast Member is carefully monitored and moved through the process so that, hopefully, that employee will one day become that shining example of guest service and Disney magic for which the Disney Corporation is so well known.

Similarly, you should approach leadership training in your church from a process point of view. When new leaders come on to your team, don't expect them to know everything from day one, even after they've completed the training. The initial training helps them learn some of the "what," but your job as a leader is to teach them, and show them, the "why." Don't view them as a finished project when the formal training ends, but, rather, a work in progress. By taking this viewpoint, you will continuously invest in those around you, rather than taking them for granted or letting them flounder on their own, as happens so often.

View every person who comes into your area of influence in the manner of the human development cycle. We all know that everyone comes into this world as an infant—helpless. As an infant we need help doing everything. As we grow, we learn to do some things by ourselves, but we still need parents and adults to teach us. The older and more mature we become, the more responsibility we are able to handle. Eventually, children grow to the point where they are ready to go out on their own. As they continue to grow, children will one day become the ones who teach and mentor others.

I think it's safe to say that we're all familiar with this life-cycle concept. Even if you have no children, you lived that life cycle. Use the life-cycle process with your church and ministry teaching. New persons who come into your church are infants. They may be infants in their faith, or they may be spiritually mature but infants in your church culture. The latter will have a much shorter learning curve. Develop an intentional cycle in your ministry to grow each person from infant to child to fully mature adult.

Don't deploy "infants" in your church on their own in any situation. Even if they are spiritually mature, they must still assimilate into the culture that you've intentionally created. Once "infants" reach "children" status, you can give more responsibility, but continue to mentor and guide. Once they are ready, send them out into their own ministry. Eventually they will be the ones mentoring others. When they become mature disciples, their mission will be to reproduce and make more disciples in whatever area God calls them.

People want to help. They want to make a difference. Your job as a leader is to develop them and give them the skills to accomplish what God has called them to do. Make sure you have a process firmly in place to accomplish that task. I used the "story" of a child growing up to convey the point. You don't have to use that specific story, but connect your process to some kind of story that enables those you are mentoring to see how they fit into the process and where they are trying to go.

Disney is big on stories. They connect everything they do to a story. If they want to motivate Cast Members to better customer service, they tell stories of how exceeding guest expectations has resulted in making a difference in the life of a child. If they want to emphasize safety, they can tell many stories about what happens when you aren't fanatical about safety details.

Recently I was speaking to a young man in one of my classes about his call to ministry. He felt frustrated that he could "never preach like my pastor." So, I told him my own story. When I was a college freshman, like him, I was brand new to the entire Christian faith. When I accepted the call to ministry as a college junior, I was still clueless about so many things, but I had grown. I look back now at some of the first sermons I preached and I cringe, but it's all part of the growing process. I tried to use my story to help him see that he shouldn't expect himself to be "SuperPastor" at age eighteen.

Similarly, many lay leaders may feel frustrated about not having seminary training. You may feel you don't know enough of the Bible, or you feel inadequate to tell anyone how to grow closer to Christ when you feel so messed up yourself, at times. That's okay. You're a work in progress. We all are. God uses a crock-pot to make us more like Christ, not a microwave. Share with your upcoming leaders how God has developed you.

By plugging into your own story, you can help new leaders to find some patience. Help them to see that you weren't always the great leader you are today. Give them encouragement and invest yourself in the process of their development. By doing this, you will ensure the success of your ministry team for years to come. In the United Methodist Church, no one is allowed to stay on a committee for more than three years at a time. If my leaders didn't invest themselves in training the next generation, we would never accomplish anything. By the time one group learns what they're doing, they rotate off. However, when the leaders take the time to constantly grow new leaders, our leadership transfer each year is fairly painless and seamless. Those leaders intentionally reproduce themselves in the next generation by passing on the DNA of the mission and vision.

GET THE RIGHT PEOPLE ON THE BUS

Jim Collins, in *Good to Great*, says that great leaders know how to get the right people in the right seats on the right bus, and the wrong people off the bus.[9] That's quite a juggling act. You might have someone who is highly talented or well trained, but their personality doesn't fit the team. You might have someone who's extremely friendly, but completely unorganized. Training and development can only go so far. You have to make sure that you have the right people in the right position to succeed. In regards to the mistake of putting someone in the wrong place, Ron Hunter and Michael Waddell write, "Not only have we just placed a round peg in a square hole, but we have limited her potential and impaired her desire for longevity with the company. People can be trained to do something outside their talents, but relegating them to that role is strategic failure."[10]

This last statement is why so many church leaders find themselves frustrated. Perhaps your pastor asked you to fill a role. You knew nothing about the position you were asked to fill, but you support your pastor and serve God and your church in any way you can. Let's assume you receive adequate training, yet you still feel frustrated; you feel like something is missing. How likely is it that you will have an effective, long-lasting ministry under these circumstances? Not likely. As a faithful servant, you'll serve the time you agreed to, but then you will drop out of leadership. The next time the pastor asks you to serve in a position of leadership, you'll be a little more hesitant. I consistently see this situation occurring in churches.

Here's some free advice: If you're not passionate about, or gifted for, an area of service, don't serve. You do yourself and your church harm by leading in an area where God did not design you to lead. Help your pastor to know where you do fit. Let him or her know that you're very willing to serve, but you want to serve in the right area where you can be most effective and satisfied.

This same advice applies when you are recruiting people to your leadership team. Don't ask someone just because you like that person. Make sure he or she has the right gifts and passion to serve in your area of ministry.

The rub with this kind of advice is: "What do I do when my denominational hierarchy requires a position to be filled and no one is passionate/gifted enough to fill that position?" My answer is to get creative. Do some Blue Sky thinking. Maybe you can rewrite the job description of that position to better fit someone's passion and gifts. You can also talk, or have the pastor talk, to the denominational hierarchy about the situation. Explain to them the vision you have for your ministry teams and why you're leaving that slot unfilled. If it is necessary (all district superintendents and bishops need to skip this sentence and go to the next paragraph), fill the slot with a name, do the best you can, but don't devote a lot of resources to that position. If it doesn't fit within your scheme of ministry and you can't find a creative solution to make it work, then just do the best you can, but don't worry about it too much.

Disney screens its Cast Members extensively for just this reason. Disney hires all types of people, but they are not going to put someone "on stage" (those who interact with guests) if they have a "backstage" (those who don't interact with guests) personality. Not everyone can stand working an entire day in a Mickey costume bringing love and happiness to hundreds of children. It takes a special person to be a character. It takes just the right kind of person to work a cash register or be a photographer. What might be a dream to one person is a nightmare to another. Disney is highly selective about whom they place in each position, and you should be, too.

At one of my previous churches I found someone with immense creative talent. She was musical and artistic and could dream huge dreams. I thought she was the perfect person to lead our worship planning team.

Too late, I found out she had absolutely no leadership skills. She was completely disorganized and chaos was erupting in the meetings as some of the stronger personalities tried to take over. I learned in a hurry that being incredibly gifted in one area does not make you suitable for leadership. So I asked if she would mind no longer leading the team, but, instead, overseeing the implementation. I thought she was going to kiss me out of relief. Because of her loyalty to me and to the church she didn't want to say no, but she also was incredibly stressed because her gifts were not in the area I was asking her to work. I found someone with strong leadership skills and good organization to run the meeting and allowed my former chairperson to lead the implementation aspect, when we did the actual painting, rehearsing, and the like. From that point on, the team flourished.

The lesson here: don't assume someone will be a good leader for a certain team just because that person is passionate about the subject. Sometimes a person will eventually make a good leader but, as mentioned before, may need development. Others may have wonderful gifts, but no matter how much training they receive they will never be good leaders. You know your ministry team and its needs better than anyone, including the pastor. It's your responsibility to ensure that the next generation of leaders will carry on the great work. How? By getting the right people into the right positions.

TRAIN TO LISTEN

I love the Garfield cartoons. Recently I saw a strip where Garfield is talking to his teddy bear, Pookie. Through each frame Garfield says, "Sigh. Pookie, Liz is nagging me about my weight. Odie won't stop barking. Jon won't stop whining. And you . . ." There is a frame where Garfield stares at Pookie. In the next frame he gives Pookie a big hug and says, "You always know just what to say."[11] Pookie, of course, didn't say a word. All he did was listen. My clinical pastoral education supervisor called it the "ministry of presence."[12]

One of the key components for any leader is the ability to listen. James 1:19 encourages believers to "let everyone be quick to listen, slow to speak, slow to anger." You, as a leader in your church, need to possess this skill, but you also need to train those you are mentoring in this skill as well. Listening is a learned skill. It is not natural. Most humans tend to think about what they are going to say next while someone is talking instead of listening closely to what the person is saying. I have occasionally, and correctly, been accused by my wife at times of "not listening" even though I could repeat every word she said. The only way to overcome this unfortunate habit is training.

Steven Covey writes that many leaders have a habit of prescribing solutions before they fully understand the problem.[13] From personal experience and observation, I agree with that statement 100 percent. All leaders want to be seen as solution finders, whether we're talking about pastors, laity, in the business world, or on a sports field. It's easy to throw out a generic solution and pat yourself on the back, but if you want to truly help solve a problem, you must first understand the problem. Would you want a doctor to give you a diagnosis before ever listening to your symptoms? The only way to understand a problem is to listen. Many wise mentors have told me, "God gave you two ears and one mouth for a reason—so that you'll listen twice as much as you talk."

Jim Garlow gives two laws of leadership: You are not a leader if people don't listen to you, and when people listen to you, you are the leader.[14] I agree with Garlow's assessment. This is a matter of relational authority versus positional authority. You might have a title (positional authority) where people have to take your orders, but that doesn't make you a leader. I've often discovered the true leader in a church is not the one with the position. He or she is the one everyone listens to (relational authority).

Taking those statements as fact, we must ask, "How do I get people to listen to me?" The answer is by listening to them first. When people really feel that you care about what they have to say it's amazing how willing they are to listen to you in return. Many conflicts within the church could be avoided if people took the time to listen to each other first.

I have started a new church, new worship services, and new ministries during my career. The times I was most successful were the times I listened to the people around me before I implemented anything. My most colossal failures were invariably the times when I pushed ahead with my own thoughts without regard for anyone else. How will you ever know what people want in a new ministry if you don't ask? You can't complain that you didn't know people were unhappy about something if you never asked their opinion in the first place. In fact, you especially need to listen to those who disagree with you. Remember, even Balaam's donkey could speak the truth, and those disagreeing with you might just be speaking truth that you really need to hear. I discovered many of the objections to new ministries could be overcome by just listening. Once people felt I had genuinely listened to their opinions, they were usually willing to go along with the final decision, even if they disagreed with it. They just wanted to know I cared enough to listen.

The concept of listening is best taught through modeling. We talked earlier about the concept of "informal" training. The Imagineers have built an intentional culture of mentoring. Chuck Ballew, Senior Concept Designer for Walt Disney Imagineering, writes, "As a mentor, don't provide every answer. Rather, ask 'Why do you think it is this way?' A good mentor doesn't give answers, but helps others figure it out for themselves."[15] One of the chief reasons Imagineers have such an incredible culture of creativity is that everyone feels he or she is heard. Instead of the head honcho saying, "Here's how it will be done," the effective leader asks questions and actually values the responses. Yes, sometimes that young, new person on your committee may give an answer that makes everyone want to roll their eyes, but resist the temptation. Listen to what that person has to say. As you model the value of listening, others will feel freer to express their ideas and they will learn, even if subconsciously, that listening to others is a value that is cherished on your leadership team.

A final reason for listening is the value of stories. I've previously mentioned that people are looking for how they can connect their personal life story to the metanarrative, God's story. How can you help them connect if you don't know their stories? If you've never taken the time to hear the story of someone's journey, and understand it, then you can never understand how to most effectively connect that person to God's story. It would be like trying to finish a puzzle without knowing the shape of the piece you need.

Another component to listening to stories is that it bonds you with that person. You can learn to love any person if you take the time to listen to her or his story. When you know where someone's been, what he or she has experienced in life, suddenly the light bulb goes on in your own mind and things that might have annoyed you in the past now don't seem like such a big deal. Why? Because you understand the source of those actions. You will feel more open and free towards that person because of the mutual understanding between you, which will also allow you to become more effective in your ministry. The other person will more willingly follow you, and listen to your leadership, because you were first willing to listen to him or her.

As a leader, model listening. In this case, modeling is the best training possible. Yes, it's good to teach those you lead good listening techniques. There are plenty of seminars and websites that will give you resources on being a good listener. While information is good, seeing it in action is much more effective. When your team sees you "practicing what you preach" they will naturally adopt the same attitude, just like everything else in your intentionally created culture.

CONCLUSION

The effectiveness of your training program will determine the effectiveness of your people. You may have more leadership knowledge than anyone else on earth, but if you don't pass that knowledge on, then, in my opinion, you have been a failure as a leader. The true measure of success as a leader is how well you reproduce yourself. Intentional training will ensure effective leadership now, during your time, as well as into the future. That way everything you start now will last long beyond your time.

Chuck Ballew describes how this works in the Disney culture perfectly: "Walt Disney continues to mentor all of us, through the stories we hear and read about him. Walt believed in the generosity, optimism, and the goodness of human beings. Mentoring involves giving, the need to respect people and embrace the bonds of humans."[16] Walt has been gone forty years and yet the impact of his leadership is still being felt. This is because he trained those around him to carry on his legacy well beyond his time. Can you say the same?

★

LIVING INTO THE LESSON

1. What do your ministry members do instinctively? What does that say about who you are?

2. How do you hold your team members or church members accountable for connecting people to God?

3. Talk about your safety plans and training for your church or ministry. Where do you need more plans and training?

4. How do you usually find your new leaders? How would mentoring someone from within change and improve your leadership training and ministry?

5. What are some ideas for "Take 5s" and "Magical Moments" within your church or ministry? How can you begin training for and implementing them? How do you think they will impact people's lives?

6. How can you be more intentional about explaining "why" in your training?

7. Think through your story and journey and share how God has developed you.

8. Have you ever served in an area that was just wrong for you? What was it like? In what areas are you most gifted to serve?

9. Talk about a time where the "ministry of presence" made a difference for you.

10. How well do you listen and train others to listen? How can you be more intentional about creating an environment of listening?

SIX ★ THE EPCOT CHURCH

We keep moving forward, opening new doors,
and doing new things, because we're curious and curiosity
keeps leading us down new paths.

—WALT DISNEY

Innovation is a subject that has been at the heart of the Disney Corporation since its inception. Walt was a firm believer in the future of humanity and wanted to be involved in bringing about that future in as many ways as possible. At a Walt Disney World gift shop I saw a t-shirt quoting Walt as saying, "Today we are the shapers of the world of tomorrow." Walt lived by the idea that what he did today would make tomorrow better for others. His constant drive to innovate came from this self-narrative that he could help make the world better through innovation. Walt's fascination with innovation showed up throughout his teachings, his inventions, and his attractions.

One of the greatest innovations made by Walt and the Imagineers is the audio-animatronic. Walt saw a mechanical bird while on vacation in Europe in the early 1950s and was inspired to create lifelike robotic creatures and people to use in his show. The first such show premiered in Disneyland in 1963 as the Enchanted Tiki Room. In 1964, Walt premiered the first human audio-animatronics at the World's Fair in New York City with Abraham Lincoln. That figure incorporated fifty-seven moves. In order to make the figure work, animator Wathel Rogers was rigged with a harnesslike device that would capture and record his every movement. This system was the earliest ancestor of the motion capture systems in use today.

At the 1964 World's Fair, Walt also premiered what he deemed his favorite attraction of all time: the Carousel of Progress. The Carousel of Progress, by itself, is a technological wonder as it consists entirely of audio-animatronics. There are no live actors involved in the show. The preshow announcement to the current version of the Carousel of Progress claims that it is the longest-running stage show, with the most performances, in the history of American theater. This attraction presented Walt's dream for a better tomorrow and his devotion to constant innovation. It follows a "typical" American family through various decades, showing how technology has improved their life. The show has been updated five times (1967, 1975, 1981, 1985, and 1994) to keep it in line with Walt's vision of the future. While the Carousel of Progress seems a little dated now, it's still one of the favorite rides for my family. Today's world has become jaded on the concept of a "great big beautiful tomorrow," and I want my boys to catch that vision.

Walt's love of innovation went well beyond the attractions for the parks. Epcot was initially EPCOT, the Experimental Prototype Community of Tomorrow. Walt's vision was for EPCOT to be a city where the latest and greatest technological advances were made a part of everyday life for those living there. Eventually, the city idea went away and EPCOT became a theme park, but the vision didn't entirely die. The initial rides of Epcot included World of Motion, Horizons, Journey Into Imagination, World of Energy, the Land, and the Living Seas. In each of those pavilions, EPCOT focused on a way to make the world a better place. Though several of those rides are now gone or modified from their original design, Epcot still serves as a showcase for innovation. For instance, the Behind the Seeds tour at the Land pavilion will allow guests to see the latest advances in crop growing techniques. Innoventions allows guests to try out new technologies, such as the Segway. The Seas with Nemo gives guests the opportunity to learn about the latest conservation efforts in the oceans.

EPCOT's original meaning, to me, is exactly what the church should be: an Experimental Prototype Community of Tomorrow. Walt's idea that we are to be "shapers of the world of tomorrow" is exactly what Jesus called the church to do. Christians are not "normal" human beings. We've been changed through a relationship with God. The church is supposed to show the world what the future will look like when Christ returns once and for all. In 1 Peter 2:11, Peter refers to Christians as "aliens and exiles" on Earth. In Philippians 3:20, Paul says that, for Christians, "our citizenship is in heaven." In John 17:16, Jesus says, in reference to his followers, "They do not belong to the world, just as I do not belong to the world." Webster's Dictionary defines "alien" as "belonging or relating to another person, place, or thing; otherworldly; differing in nature or character, typically to the point of incompatibility; a resident of another home, country, or planet."[1]

We can take this idea of "incompatibility" and being "aliens" one of two ways. The first would be that Christians are outcasts. The world has shunned us, so we should simply circle the wagons and wait for Christ to return. The second view is that Christians are innovators. We should be leading the charge for change in the world. The first view has the entire world against Christianity. It's an Us versus Them mentality. There is certainly some truth to that. Just read *Foxe's Book of Martyrs* and you'll see in a hurry that many people are still persecuted because of their faith in Jesus. It's true that Christians are sometimes looked down upon or made fun of due to their beliefs. In many parts of the world, Christians are still dying for their faith. Does this mean Jesus wants us to group together in a holy huddle to await his return? Did the early church give up because a couple of crazy emperors were killing every Christian they could find?

In John 18:36, Jesus told Pilate, "My kingdom is not from this world." Jesus' greatest message throughout his time on Earth is that God's realm, or the kingdom of God, had come among us (compare Luke 17:21, Luke 10:9, Matt. 12:28). Throughout Jesus' many references to the kingdom of God, the Greek language expresses a now and not yet concept. God's reign is on Earth now, but its fullness won't be seen until Christ returns. That means the Christian community is supposed to show the world now what the entire world will look like then. Jesus makes very clear that he does not intend for Christians to retreat into a fortress to await his coming. John 17:15 says, "I am not asking you to take them out of the world, but I ask you to protect them from the evil one." In Acts 1 and Matthew 28, Jesus sends the apostles to the entire world. In Matthew 5:13, Jesus says, "You are the salt of the earth" and, in verse 14, "You are the light of the world." He specifically instructs his followers in verses 15–16 to not hide their light, but, instead, "In the same way, let your light shine before others, so that they may see your good works and give glory to your Father in heaven."

I've taken the time for this mini–Bible study to show you that Jesus never intended his church to exist for its own benefit, nor hide away behind closed doors. William Temple, Archbishop of Canterbury during World War II, said, "The Church is the only society that exists for the benefit of those who are not its members."[2] It's not "Us versus Them" but "Us for Them." If we, as the community of Christ, are supposed to exist for those outside our doors, then we must become innovators. We are to show those in the world what a new life can be like and what God's realm will be like when Christ returns. We are to live now as if he has already returned. We live the life of the future in the present. In other words, we become a true EPCOT.

BACK TO THE FUTURE

By definition, being the Experimental Prototype Community of Tomorrow means showing the world today what the world of tomorrow is supposed to look like. The church has a bit of a problem with accomplishing this task. If you asked the average Joe on the street where the hippest, most cutting-edge place in town could be found, I seriously doubt someone would mention a local church, no matter how many people you asked. And that's okay. I have some serious reservations about churches that are constantly trying to keep up with the cultural trends. But being an EPCOT church doesn't mean that we keep up with all of the latest fads. Paul reminds Christians in Romans 12:2 to not "be conformed to this world, but be transformed by the renewing of your minds." In my understanding, this means don't try to copy everything the culture does. The church should be separate from the world. We just can't be so alien in our way of doing things that an unchurched person has problems finding a point of connection. This is a fine line to walk. On one hand, we want to be relevant and speak to the needs of the world around us. On the other hand, we don't want our path to be dictated by every shift in the fads of culture. Our path is to be guided by the Spirit of God, not the whims of the world.

Most Christians now recognize that the world around us has changed. I see the vast majority of churches responding to this realization in one of three ways. First, they circle the wagons, dig in their heels, and say, "We've always done it this way and we're not going to change." Those churches will either change or die within a few years. Then I see churches at the other extreme doing everything they can to be "edgy" and "hip." Those churches will suffer a serious identity crisis when what they now think is "hip" is no longer relevant. The third response, and the most common one, is a church that wants to engage its culture, but also wants to be faithful to its Christian roots—but doesn't really know how to do either. In that situation, these people tend to try whatever programming fad is going around at the moment in an effort to find something that works.

The most visible example of these three scenarios is worship. In example one you have faithful believers who are worshiping the way they have since before their grandparents. The narrative of their church is that in order to honor God we have to do the right things in the right way. To change the way we do things would be seen as invalidating our past, and we cherish our past too much to do that. This is the church where, except for the cars parked out front, you wouldn't be able to tell whether the year is 1900, 1950, or 2010. The most recent song would probably be something written by the Gaithers in the 1970s. Outside of that, the church will not have changed the way they worship in generations.

The second example would mostly consist of very young churches (by age of the church, not necessarily the age of the worshipers). Their narrative is that the "old" way of doing church is broken. They desperately want to engage a world that has largely rejected Christianity. In order to do this, they use the music, images, styles, and language of the culture around them in their worship services. To this group, the past is an anchor that drags the church down. In the previous example, the past is an anchor that keeps the church secure through the storms of life. I hope you are beginning to see how the story of your church and life largely affects how you relate to God.

Our third example is a church that probably has multiple services. They'll have at least one traditional service, but have also started a "contemporary" service to try to engage the current culture. The narrative of this church is a strong belief in preserving the past, but also wanting to ensure the future.

The reason I put the word contemporary in quotes is that what most churches are passing off as contemporary in 2011 is really a thirty- to forty-year-old concept. I don't know of anyone who considers something forty years old as contemporary, yet that's what we call it in the church. When a church says it has a contemporary worship service, it's usually just as traditional as the "traditional" service. The elements are slightly different, but nine times out of ten I know what to expect before I walk through the door. Most people will be wearing business casual clothing (khaki pants and a golf shirt for the men, slacks and a comfortable blouse for the women) instead of the suits and dresses typical in the traditional service. There will definitely be coffee served before and during the service, and possibly some doughnuts or other light snacks. The service will consist of twenty to thirty minutes of singing "contemporary" praise choruses and songs. There will usually be a worship leader and praise band who will sing a solo related to the message during the offertory, then the pastor will preach for about thirty minutes. There will definitely be a screen with images or movie clips projected during the sermon. Some elements may slightly vary from week to week and church to church but, in essence, that's what you find in every contemporary service.

That entire concept was started by the Jesus People movement on the West Coast in the 1970s and gained serious traction with the seeker-sensitive movement of the 1980s.[3] The format has changed very little, yet we still call it "contemporary" and some churches are just now trying to start this thirty-plus-year-old model as a way of reaching modern culture.

What I have found interesting over my years of ministry is that most people care very little about the style of worship. These worship wars being fought within our churches are, for the most part, a waste of time. We're fighting about the wrong things. In my personal research, I have found that people want three things out of a worship experience. First, they want relevant, biblically based preaching. They want to hear what God has to say for their lives that week. Good preaching should not be entertainment, but it should use the metaphors and imagery of the world to show where God connects. Second, they want to worship in a place where, as the *Cheers* theme song said, "everybody knows your name." They want to feel welcomed, accepted, and wanted. Finally, they want to encounter God; to connect to something bigger than themselves. You can accomplish all three of these things in every style of worship. If you will take the time to explain the rituals and their meanings, most people will be content in any style of worship as long as those three requirements are met.

If worship style really doesn't matter, why do churches make such a big deal about it? Mostly, I think, because it's the most visible thing we do as a community of faith. A contemporary, or postmodern, worship service does not make your church an EPCOT church any more than having a traditional worship style makes you irrelevant. For many people, worship is the only connection with the church on a weekly basis, so that is where the most emotional energy is invested. But, as we will explore later in this chapter, you can be an EPCOT church regardless of worship style.

The buzzword I'm hearing more in worship discussion circles is "ancient-future," also sometimes referred to as "vintage Christianity."[4] The idea behind this movement is to connect with the ancient roots of the church while staying relevant to the current culture. It's a both/and approach. In most cases, regardless of style, the worship service has been used to elicit an emotional response and dispense information to the congregation. The congregation is generally passive: sitting or standing as a band, pastor, and PowerPoint dictate their spiritual response. The idea of ancient-future worship is to design worship so that it intentionally tells God's story and connects the participants to that story using a variety of methods, both old and new. The ancient-future concept is resonating with many people because it helps them to connect to something bigger than themselves and to feel a part of the two thousand years of church history, but in a way that is meaningful today.

This last statement is what being an EPCOT church is really about. When Walt Disney envisioned the future, he never thought of discarding the past. Rather, he built on that past. Churches that discard their heritage, the foundation of their faith, will find themselves tossed about by whatever comes along. Churches that dig in their heels and never move forward will find themselves nothing more than a living museum to a previous era. It's the balancing act that is so important.

Dan Kimball is right on target when he says, "When we hear that cultural changes are occurring, our initial reaction may be to try to pinpoint the new problems and then tweak our ministries to fix them."[5] By reacting in this manner, however, we are missing the fundamental question: Is our current way of connecting people to God working? We assume that all we need to do is tweak, but we may need a major overhaul. If you're going to be successful, you must look at all of your ministries and decide which is needed: minor tweaks or major overhaul. Disney does this on a regular basis with their attractions. Every so often, an attraction is taken offline for maintenance and refurbishment. But, Disney is constantly asking whether they should clean up and maintain what they already have or completely overhaul the experience for something new.

Up until now, I've given plenty of examples about the excellence of Disney, but the Disney Corporation has not always followed this balancing act so well. One of the best examples is the Imagination pavilion in Epcot. The pavilion first opened as Journey Into Imagination in 1982 and featured Figment and Dreamfinder, who instantly became well-loved Disney characters. The ride was a smash hit and loved by most everyone of my generation, who were kids when the pavilion first opened. In 1997, Fujifilm came to Disney offering to make Journey Into Imagination into a thrill ride that had nothing to do with imagination. Kodak, the original pavilion sponsor, was about to lose out on their sponsorship deal. They proposed to make Journey Into Imagination into something more scientific. The ride would also be shorter and have cheaper special effects. Because a thrill ride would be much more expensive to maintain, Disney accepted Kodak's idea and overhauled Journey Into Imagination, which reopened as Journey Into Your Imagination in 1999. The story now focused on the Imagination Institute with Dr. Nigel Channing. Dreamfinder was completely cut out, the original theme song, "One Little Spark," was changed, and Figment only made a short cameo at the end. The fans were outraged.

Part of the magic of Disney is that I grew up with the Walt Disney Parks and now I can take my children back to enjoy the same experiences I had. It thrills me to take my boys on the rides I loved so much as a child and watch them experience the magic. It's almost like being a kid again myself. So, when Disney took away something so many of my age group loved as children, it almost felt like we lost part of our childhood. There was a very emotional reaction and guests boycotted the new ride and Kodak products as a result.

In October 2001, Disney closed the Imagination pavilion again and reopened it on June 1, 2002, as Journey Into Imagination with Figment. Dreamfinder was still missing, but Figment had reappeared with a much more prominent role and a new storyline. The fans are still clamoring for the return of Dreamfinder, and the Internet Disney message boards continue discussions around rumors that a true Journey Into Imagination pavilion will one day return, but most fans are happy to see Figment back.

Let me now give you a positive example. In 2007, Walt Disney World closed the Haunted Mansion for a major refurbishment. The Haunted Mansion is one of Disney's most well-known and loved attractions. In this case, Disney made Madam Leota's crystal ball seem to float, instead of sitting on the table as before, enhanced the staircase with new effects, and made the attic scene much more entertaining. The graveyard effects were also updated to give more of a "wow" feeling and less of a carnival sideshow as the previous effects had done. When the ride reopened it was met with rave reviews. Why? Because Disney kept everything people loved and remembered, but also enhanced and added to the attraction at the same time. There have been no cries on the message boards for Disney to return the Haunted Mansion to its original state because in making changes they stayed true to what the fans loved.

These two stories illustrate just how tough it can be to innovate when you also have to balance tradition. Fans want new rides and experiences, but they also don't want to give up their childhood memories. They want that connection to the past while being given new and innovative experiences.

The church faces the same dilemma. I have found that many people who have drifted away from church attendance tend to return when they have children of their own. For whatever reason, they didn't feel church was necessary or relevant while they were young adults or newly married, but once children enter the picture they long for their kids to have the same experience that they did.

When they return to church, they want to find it like they remember it. It's an issue of comfort and familiarity. Life changes so rapidly, and the storms of life can rock you to your very foundation, so people want to know that some things are stable. For most people, they remember church as "safe" and "fun" from when they were children. Whether they understood everything going on in worship or not, they remember friends from Sunday school and friendly adults who helped them learn about God. The familiar elements of worship and of the church in general help people connect to those feelings from their childhood. They gain some sense of stability in the midst of a rapidly changing world. So, the question becomes, "Can stability and innovation coexist?" Yes! As demonstrated above, Disney doesn't always get it right, but they are the perfect example of how you can connect people to the memories of their past while continuing to do new things.

Being an EPCOT church has very little to do with worship style. It's all about demonstrating what God's realm looks like. All churches can accomplish that in their own unique way. Your church's story is just one part of God's story. The balance is in keeping your church's story connected to the entirety of God's story—past, present, and future. Over the rest of this chapter we'll explore the principles behind being innovative while not losing that connection to your heritage.

WHAT'S STOPPING YOU?

Before we talk about how to be innovative, let's first ask, "What's stopping us from being innovative now?" I can sum it up in one word: comfort. You need to honestly ask, "How willing am I to be uncomfortable in order to help my church be an EPCOT church?" No one enjoys being uncomfortable. We usually go out of our way to avoid discomfort. However, change does not happen without some level of pain. Great leaders are willing to take that next step, even when it hurts.

Maxie Dunnam was president of Asbury Theological Seminary in Wilmore, Kentucky, while I was there working on my master's degree. I remember him saying during a sermon in chapel, "People would rather stay in the hell of the known than risk the potential heaven of the unknown." This is exactly what stops us from being EPCOT churches! You might have noticed that I have, as of yet, not defined exactly what an EPCOT church looks like. That is intentional. It'll look different in every situation. The common factor is asking, "When Christ returns, what will the world look like?" and then living that out within your community of faith. But that is very different from the way the world is now. To live in such a countercultural way risks ridicule, rejection, and discomfort. The reward is seeing lives changed beyond anything you can possibly imagine. I think all of us would love to see the latter happen in our churches. It is the risk that stops us.

If we're honest, we also have to say that we're somewhat lazy. I have never met a person who didn't believe that being in excellent physical shape is a good thing. We're also all equally capable of being in good shape by eating healthily and getting the proper amount of exercise. Even most people with physical limitations are capable of some types of exercise and watching their diet. So if we all believe in it and we're all capable of accomplishing it, why isn't everyone in good shape? Because we're lazy. Being in good physical shape means I can't eat whatever I want when I want. It means I have to stress the muscles of my body, which is painful. It means I have to change my daily routine, which I don't like. All of these things lead to most people saying, "Being in shape is a good thing, but it's just too uncomfortable to do it."

Churches act the same way. We all believe that seeing lives changed is a good thing. We all believe that being devoted to Bible study, prayer, and worship will help us grow more like Christ. But we don't want to give up our comfort to make those things happen. We like worship done our way, with the programs we like, at the time we want. In short, we're self-focused. Being an EPCOT church means you live focused on others. The realm of God is about serving others, not being served. Read John 13 if you want Jesus' opinion on the matter.

Being the Experimental Prototype Community of Tomorrow means we're the example. We get to show everyone now what life will be like then. To live in this manner, we need to take some risks, make some changes, and deal with any discomfort it might cause us. You, as the leader, need to model this attitude. How will it be necessary for you to sacrifice your personal comfort to help your church achieve its goals? How can you lead others through this discomfort and on towards your goals? It'll all be worth it in the end.

Before I became a pastor I was a meteorologist. One of the most fascinating aspects of studying weather came from the study of hurricanes. Every hurricane goes through a cycle called eye-wall replacement. The storm grows and then plateaus in strength. Once the storm hits the plateau, eye-wall replacement begins. During eye-wall replacement the storm is reorganizing itself and will appear to weaken. One of two things will happen during the cycle: the storm will completely fall apart or the storm will emerge stronger than ever. This is how hurricanes grow. They constantly reorganize and emerge stronger or they die.

The church needs to undergo eye-wall replacement every so often. When our vision becomes ragged, our focus not as tight, then we must reorganize or die. This is where the discomfort comes in. We might have to let some things we like go in order to refocus on our vision. We might also have to fight for some of our ideas to see them come to fruition. Jeff Larson, vice-president of global marketing for the Disney parks, said that if you want your ideas to succeed at Disney, you have to be willing to fight for them. If the idea isn't worth fighting for, then it's not worth spending money to do.[6] Are you passionate enough about your ideas to fight to make them happen? Sure, it's uncomfortable to engage in conflict, but that's part of the growing process.

Lee Cockerell quotes from the Disney Great Leader Strategies, "In times of drastic change, it is the learners who inherit the future. The learned usually find themselves equipped to live in a world that no longer exists."[7] I can't think of a better quote to sum up what it takes to be an EPCOT church. Those who open their minds to the possibilities that exist in Christ, those who are willing to take the risks to achieve great things for God, will be the ones who see their goals realized. The ones who risk the most will see the greatest reward and show the world what it truly means to live as part of the coming reign of God today.

LIFETIME LEARNER

Now we turn our attention to the burning question: how? How do I become an innovator and help my church become an EPCOT church? You start by becoming a lifetime learner. You've already taken one step by purchasing this book. My purpose in writing this book is not to give you all of the answers, but, hopefully, to stoke in you the fire of creativity. Since every person reading this book will be in a different situation, there is no way that I could cover all the possible scenarios and ways of doing things. But I can give you principles that you can then figure out how to apply specifically in your situation.

The more you learn, the greater the chances of success. Never stop learning. It breaks my heart that I can walk into the office of many pastors and with just a glance at their bookshelves I know when they graduated from seminary. How? They haven't bought any new books since. There are so many books, articles, and conferences available to you that to not take advantage of them is a waste of the ability God gave you. The Internet is full of leadership blogs and articles. The bookstores are stocked with more leadership books than you can imagine. There is a conference going on somewhere almost every week. If you're interested in learning more about Disney, read the books I've quoted from in their entirety. They're all great books and will expand your knowledge base.

The question has been raised, "How do I know the good books from the bad ones?" That's a good question. If you're like me, you don't have a lot of extra time to waste on something that is not worthwhile. Just using Google, or some other search engine, is often unsatisfactory because you will be overwhelmed with choices without any sense of how to evaluate what's before you. You'll have to find a system that works for you in separating the good from the bad, but allow me to share with you my process. I start by asking those I respect what they're reading and have found useful. I look for blogs of authors I respect and see who they are reading or quoting. Often blogs will have links to other blogs. If one author is useful, then you can plug into the ones he or she has found useful. I read reviews online to see what others have said about a book, and I check out the endorsements. If I've never heard of an author, but I see that someone I respect has endorsed this new author, then I'll give that author a chance. So, in essence, I find good, new resources by playing connect-the-dots. Sometimes I'll pick up something that has no endorsements, I've never heard of the author, and it turns out to be great. In those situations, I generally try to read a chapter in the bookstore and skim through the rest of the book before I actually purchase it. Whatever system you use for finding new resources, make sure you're doing it. Finding new books and blogs is one of the best ways to stretch your mind and expand your ministry. And don't read only those books that present a viewpoint you totally agree with. Sometimes you need opposing viewpoints to help you better understand your own. Contrary thoughts can often be the ones that lead to the best learning experiences.

In being a learner, use both secular and church conferences. I always enjoy the Willow Creek Leadership Summit. Usually it's held around the first of August each year, both live in Chicago and in simulcast around the country.[8] The summit intentionally brings together some of the greatest Christian leadership minds, such as Adam Hamilton, Erwin McManus, and Andy Stanley, together with some of the greatest corporate leadership minds, such as Jim Collins and Patrick Lencioni. In a short time you get to hear from the best of both worlds.

Leadership Nexus does a Creative Ministry Conference each winter in Orlando, bringing in some of the best Disney people to talk about using Disney ideas in your church.[9] The Disney Institute offers tremendous leadership programs.[10] Church of the Resurrection, outside of Kansas City, offers a Leadership Institute that is especially good for those of you in a more traditional church setting.[11] I've mentioned just four conferences. There are many, many more. And, contrary to popular belief, these conferences are not aimed only at pastors. Every one of these conferences is open to, and beneficial for, both laity and clergy.

There's no excuse for not being a lifetime learner. The resources are all around you. It only takes you making the effort to access those resources. Innovation is part of Disney's culture. So is learning. You can't separate the two. If you want to be innovative and bring people to God in new ways, you have to feed your brain through learning.

KNOW YOUR PEOPLE

Disney uses the term "Guestology" to refer to studying what their guests want, what the demographics are, how the trends are shifting, and so on. Disney knows their market. They are constantly adjusting their marketing strategies and park policies based on the information they gather.[12]

You also need to study the culture around you if you're going to successfully connect those people to God. When Disney decides to build a new ride, they don't randomly choose a theme. Disney decided to go with a Pixie Hollow area in Fantasyland because the pixies are all the rage with little girls right now. Then they rethought that decision because they realized that most of who comes to Walt Disney World are families, not just little girls. As a result, they wanted to do something more family oriented.

I am not, in any way, suggesting a consumer-oriented approach to church. I'm not saying that you should make your worship time an entertainment spectacle and play the music heard on the local Top 40 radio station. I'm not saying give in to every demand of the world around you. What I am saying is you have to know who the people are in your community if you're going to know how best to connect them to Jesus.

The message of Jesus doesn't change, but the methods must. If your church attempts to reach a twenty-first-century world using early twentieth-century methods, you'll fail miserably. I've heard some use Hebrews 13:8 as an excuse: "Jesus Christ is the same yesterday and today and forever." That's quite correct. The character of Jesus never changes, but the methods of conveying the love of Christ must change.

If Disney never built a new attraction or, worse yet, built new attractions using only 1950s technology, they would not create much excitement. When they find a new movie that's a hit, you can bet they will find a way for those characters to show up in the parks. Disney's bottom line depends on understanding what their target audience wants.

Well, how do you find those answers? You do it through "Guestology" —the study of the guests. One way is to do "man on the street" interviews. Take your ministry team one Saturday down to a local hang-out, whether a park, a ball field, a restaurant, or wherever is "the" place in your community. Take a survey asking the people what they're looking for in a church. Be sure to ask them if they are currently active in a church so that you can categorize the responses. Are you targeting those already with a church home or those with no connection? Your response to that question will tell you which set of answers you should use to guide your planning and visioning.

There are also demographic resources available. Search the U.S. Census bureau. The data is readily available.[13] Percept is a company that packages the census data for your specifically defined area (zip code, radius from your location, and so on) with specific issues for churches. Several denominations have contracts with Percept to allow their churches to use the Link2Lead site at no cost to the church. City-Data is another site that can give you a breakdown of your community at no cost. It's general information, not specific to churches, but the information can be very useful in reaching your community.[14]

Your next question might be, "How do I make use of this data?" First, do a census of your church and examine the demographics. What's the median age? What are the primary concerns? Where is the average income level? Once you have that snapshot of the church, compare it to the data found about your community. If your church doesn't reflect the community, ask yourself why not. What is it about your church that gives it a different demographic than the community surrounding it? Is that a good thing or a bad thing? Do you want your church to reflect the community at large, or are you targeting a specific group of people? Maybe your ministry team is only targeting youth or children. In that case, are there a lot of families in your area with teenagers or children? If not, then you need to change your focus.

Other than looking at your own congregation, another way to make use of this data is in planning for your new ministries. To use the idea above, if there are no children in your community, then doing Vacation Bible School might not be the best use of resources. If there are no retirees, then doing a retirement planning seminar wouldn't get you very far. The Percept data, especially, is helpful because it tells you the greatest concerns of those in your community in a generic sense (that is, spiritual concerns, health concerns, or children and family).

I suggest you look at the data that is available and then hold a Blue Sky session as to how your team can best use the information you find.

The possibilities are almost limitless. The point is to know who is in the community around you so that you can know how to address your needs. If you're answering questions that no one is asking, you'll never be successful.

SEPARATE FROM THE PACK

The Disney parks stand alone as the height of entertainment. While other parks may have bigger roller coasters or their own brand of shows and parades, no one has been able to successfully challenge Disney's dominance because Disney wrote the book on creating an immersive park environment. Universal Studios and SeaWorld both have parks in Orlando, but people think first of Disney because of everything Disney has done to set themselves apart as unique.

Because Disney has been around so long, almost everyone has an emotional connection to the name. That's what places them in a category all their own. Watching *Snow White, Sleeping Beauty, The Lion King,* or *Toy Story* (we could go on and on) with your children for the first time brings back all of those emotional connections from your own childhood. It is a family bonding experience that no other brand in the family-entertainment genre can even come close to competing with.

The other parks now recognize Disney's uniqueness and, mostly, don't try to compete against it in a head-to-head fashion. They've tried to find their own niche. Universal Studios has tried less to cater to families and more to the teenager/young adult crowd. It's not that they don't care about families, or don't have anything for families, but they realize Disney "owns" families and so they are trying to make their own mark. SeaWorld brings people into an encounter with marine life that is above anything any other park can offer. They are known for Shamu and up-close dolphin encounters. They've found the niche that makes them unique.

Jim Atchinson, president of SeaWorld Parks and Entertainment, said, "Theme park consumers extract value from thousands of discrete memories and experiences. Each experience adds to or detracts from a consumer's perception of value."[15] Jim understands that people don't spend thousands of dollars to ride rides. They come for the experience. Being a category of one, to use Joe Calloway's term, means you create an experience that the "consumer" (that is, the person you're trying to reach with the gospel message) can't find anywhere else.

In the church, we don't have a physical object to give people. We are an experiential entity, so how we pay attention to the experience is how people will judge the value of what we have to say. No detail of the guest experience can be considered insignificant. I can literally see three other churches from the front porch of my church. I drive past a total of twelve churches from the time I leave my office until I pull into my driveway ten minutes later. It's unfair to say that other churches are competition. We're all on the same team. I want all twelve of those churches to be successful. But in a church-saturated environment I have to ask, "What experience does my church have to offer that makes it unique?" We all talk about Jesus (hopefully). We all offer Bible study and worship. Those things aren't going to separate our church from the one down the street. I wrote previously about how I decided to make the focus of RSUMC "family." We want every person who walks through the door to feel welcomed and accepted like nowhere else. We want people to experience the unconditional love of Christ through our acceptance of them.

This issue of becoming a category of one is vital whether you are the big church on the block or a small family chapel. You're not competing with anyone else, so don't try to be like anyone else. Be the best you that you can be. Disney has never changed their formula. They add rides and experiences, but they always stay within the vision of who they are. For fifty-five years they've maintained that vision and been successful. They don't change based on what any other theme park does. They keep up with the times. They adjust to what their guests are looking for, but they don't change the core of who they are.

You may have fifty churches in a ten-mile radius of your church. It doesn't matter. What makes you unique? There are enough people who don't know Jesus personally in that ten-mile radius for all fifty churches to be packed to overflowing. So just because another church is growing does not mean your church has to feel threatened or feel like you can't grow. You can all be successful. But you have to figure out what you can offer that sets you apart from the rest.

In the South, if someone wants a soft drink, they ask for a "Coke," no matter what flavor of soft drink they actually want. If people are talking about coffee, generally the name Starbucks is mentioned. Lots of different discount airlines have popped up, yet Southwest is the one everyone mentions. If someone sees a motorcycle, what is the first brand that comes to mind? Harley-Davidson. And so it goes. Each one of those brands established itself as unique in its category and has become the name of the product. In studying each of those companies, along with Disney, I found one factor that especially stuck out: all were well-defined in identity.

When I ask a group of people to define their church's identity I usually get a lot of blank stares. It's the toughest question for churches to answer. Maybe the pastor has thought about it some, but how many of the lay people spend time thinking, "Who are we? What makes us different from everyone else?" If God can create every snowflake unique, every set of fingerprints unique, then God can certainly make every church unique. The excuse that "all the good ideas are taken" doesn't cut it. That's an excuse of laziness. If you're willing to work hard enough, to do the Blue Sky process, you can figure out your unique identity.

TO CHANGE OR NOT TO CHANGE

Change for the sake of change is a bad thing. You have to be able to answer the questions I've previously raised before you'll know if you need to change something about your church. When you have a firm idea of who you are, who the people around you are, what makes you unique, and what obstacles might present themselves in your mission, then you'll know what, if anything, to change. However, not changing just because you're comfortable is an equal threat.

I mentioned earlier how being comfortable is a threat to our ability to be innovative. An equal threat is past success because it brings on complacency. If you've been successful in your leadership at your church you might be tempted to think, "I know how to do this. I've got this leadership thing down cold." Joe Calloway is right on target when he says, "If you're successful, that means you know what used to work."[16] We must have a holy urgency about our work. There is no such thing as a retired Christian this side of heaven. Just because we've done something well in the past does not guarantee future success.

I'm not suggesting that you throw away your church's tradition or that you unlearn everything you've ever known about being a good leader in your church. I'm saying build on what you know to get better. Whether you're reading this book at age ten or age one hundred, there is something new you need to do in order to be successful in the future. That means change. "Don't make assumptions about what will work tomorrow based on what worked yesterday."[17] In other words, be intentional about deciding what methods and processes you'll use in bringing the next generation to Christ. If Sunday school and Vacation Bible School worked twenty years ago, great! Don't assume they'll work next year. Maybe it's time to switch to small groups for children and teenagers. Maybe it's time to do a Fall Festival or a Family Bible Week or something different. Build on what you know, but don't assume that relying on what you know will bring you success in the future.

IT'S ALL ABOUT PEOPLE

All the ideas and processes in the world can't replace the people. Even if you are a master strategist, help create wonderful experiences, and are a genius at innovation, what people will most remember about your church are the people. And that's the way it should be. There's a great little hymn whose refrain is "I am the church. You are the church. We are the church together." Then the first verse says, "The church is not a building, the church is not a steeple, the church is not a resting place, the church is a people."[18] The greatest innovations in the world still have to be put into action by people.

People are your greatest resource, so use them. If people are going to remember more the people involved in an experience than the program itself, spend your time thinking most about how to use your people in innovative ways. Every time we go to Disney World a Cast Member will distinguish himself or herself. Sometimes it's something very simple, like stopping to wish my son a happy birthday. Sometimes it's spending time explaining the history of the Cast Member's home country. Sometimes it's helping us figure out a dilemma. Whatever the issue, we remember

Cast Members from every single trip. My wife and I married in 1996 and took our honeymoon to Walt Disney World. We still laugh and talk about "Rosie" who was our "mom" (waitress) at the 50s Prime Time Café. Because of her, that restaurant became our family's favorite and something we have to do on pretty much every single trip. The environment of the restaurant itself is fun, but it would be worthless without the Cast Members to bring it to life. Use the people on your ministry team to their maximum effectiveness. Without them, the most innovative program in the world will still flop.

CONCLUSION

Walt Disney loved to innovate. He loved to bring people in touch with the community of tomorrow. Your church, also, should be an EPCOT church. Show the world what things will be like when God reigns supreme on earth. Jesus often uses the phrase "kingdom of God." That phrase, in the Greek, means the place in which God has ultimate authority and dominion over all things. It means, as Jesus prayed, that God's will is truly being done on earth as in heaven. If your church lives by that ideal, if you became an EPCOT church, what would that look like? I dare you to find out. You'll change the community around you more than you've ever believed possible.

★

LIVING INTO THE LESSON

1. Why do you think we as Christians should be "shapers of the world of tomorrow"? How do you envision this in action?

2. Does your church function more in the mode of "circle the wagons" or as innovators? Why?

3. The author makes the statement that "God's reign is on Earth now, but its fullness won't be seen until Christ returns." How do you, both personally and as a leader in your ministry, "show the world now what the entire world will look like then"?

4. "We, as the community of Christ, are supposed to exist for those outside our doors." How are you living this out right now? How can you better accomplish this in your ministry?

5. How does your church or ministry typically respond to our changing world?

6. How do you relate to the author's discussion of the three requirements for relevant worship? Why are these things so important to people?

7. Why do you think that connecting with our two-thousand-year church history speaks to people today?

8. How willing are you to give up what you find comfortable in order to be innovative? How has the desire for comfort or laziness limited your church/ministry's ability to change lives?

9. Are you a "lifetime learner?" What topics would help you sharpen your leadership skills?

10. How well do you know the community you are serving? What will you do to begin learning who it is you're serving?

11. What makes your church unique from all others? What do you offer that no one else does?

12. Do you effectively use those on your ministry team or do you tend to be a one-man/woman show? How can you more effectively use those who serve with you?

SEVEN ★ LIVING ONSTAGE

I am different from [George] Washington;
I have a higher, grander standard of principle.
Washington could not lie.
I can lie, but I won't."

—MARK TWAIN

One of my all-time favorite experiences at Walt Disney World is the DiveQuest tour, which takes place at the Seas with Nemo and Friends pavilion in Epcot. As part of the tour, each guest is allowed to scuba dive in the aquarium. The tour begins by taking the guests "back-stage," which is the term Disney uses to refer to any area not normally seen by guests. Following an extensive tour of the inner workings of the aquarium, each guest is given a wetsuit and brought into a long blue hallway.

The first time I entered this hallway, my son Caleb and I were doing the AquaSeas tour, which is similar to DiveQuest, but for those not scuba certified. When we entered the blue hallway our guide asked if anyone knew why the hallway was blue. Everyone assumed that it was "water" colored because of the theme of the pavilion. The Cast Member explained that throughout Walt Disney World every hallway and door that leads "onstage" (any area where a Cast Member might encounter guests) is painted blue like this to remind the Cast Members of their mission.

While backstage, Cast Members are "normal" people. They have lives outside of Disney World: bills to pay, hobbies, problems, and everything else that occurs in the lives of "normal" people. When they enter that blue hallway, or see the blue door, however, all Cast Members are expected to drop all of their problems and all of their personal issues and focus only on the mission of making people happy. A Cast Member might be so angry at her spouse that she is ready to pull out her hair. Another might be frustrated with a fellow Cast Member, or worried about his dog's surgery, but he is not allowed to have a bad day once he goes through that blue door. Once on the other side of the blue door, the Cast Member is no longer a "normal" person. He or she is a Disney Cast Member whose sole focus is to create magic in the lives of the guests encountered that day.

Being able to set aside your personal feelings in this manner takes a lot of training, but it is part of what makes the Disney magic so powerful and prevalent. I have been to amusement parks where I have encountered a surly teenager barely glancing at me as I board the ride, and an irritated older man complaining about the loud kids running around the park as he runs the cash register in a gift shop. I understand what those people are feeling. "Normal" people would be very irritated at the way some people act on vacation. I consistently encounter people at various amusement parks with very little consideration for the park workers or any other person in the park. But Disney Cast Members are not "normal."

The intense training we talked about in chapter 5 allows them to set aside any frustration, worry, or personal grievances while they are onstage and simply focus upon the guests. Cast Members aren't robots, nor are they perfect, so sometimes you'll see a little frustration when a guest is particularly challenging. However, that is the exception, not the rule. The next time you're in a Disney park and are greeted by a Cast Member with a big smile, keep in mind that that Cast Member may be going through a very rough time in life but is setting all of that aside to focus on your happiness. That realization might help you be a little more patient if that Cast Member doesn't exceed your expectations immediately.

All of Jesus' teachings, especially the Sermon on the Mount, assert that Christians are not "normal" people, either. Jesus says, "You have heard that it was said, 'You shall love your neighbor and hate your enemy.' But I say to you, Love your enemies and pray for those who persecute you, so that you may be children of your Father in heaven; for he makes his sun rise on the evil and on the good, and sends rain on the righteous and on the unrighteous. For if you love those who love you, what reward do you have? Do not even the tax collectors do the same? And if you greet only your brothers and sisters, what more are you doing than others? Do not even the Gentiles do the same?" (Matt. 5:43–47). Love your enemies? That's not normal. Jesus acknowledges that he is asking his followers to be different by saying, "Even the tax collectors and Gentiles can love those who love them, but my followers are to love even those who hate them." Jesus makes other comments about turning the other cheek when someone strikes you, and walking two miles with one who forces you to walk one. Perhaps most astounding is the scene recorded in John 13 when Jesus performs an act of service relegated only to the lowliest of slaves—foot washing. After the Lord and Creator of the universe gets up from washing the dirty feet of his followers he says, "You call me Teacher and Lord— and you are right, for that is what I am. So if I, your Lord and Teacher, have washed your feet, you also ought to wash one another's feet. For I have set you an example, that you also should do as I have done to you" (John 13:13–15). That's not normal, but that is exactly what being an EPCOT church is all about.

Disney's goal within their parks is to create an environment that allows you to forget the outside world, all your stresses and worries, for just a few hours. They take this so seriously that they even paid several million dollars to have Orange County move a huge radio tower so that it couldn't be seen from within the parks. They want nothing from the outside world to disrupt the magic. One bad encounter with a Cast Member can ruin the entire experience for the guest. So the blue doors and halls remind the Cast Members constantly of whom they represent and the attitude they need to have when they walk through that door.

I think we should paint the exit doors to our churches blue. The church should be safe place where you can feel free to be yourself, warts and all, so that together we can learn to be more like Christ. Now, I realize that's a little idealistic and that, in reality, church is usually the place where people put on their masks and act as if everything is fine and perfect. Our goal, however, should be to make the church a place where you can have the freedom to "work out your own salvation" (Phil. 2:12) so that when we exit the church and our homes we are "onstage" representing Christ. Jesus said in Matthew 5:14–16, "You are the light of the world. A city built on a hill cannot be hid. No one after lighting a lamp puts it under the bushel basket, but on the lampstand, and it gives light to all in the house. In the same way, let your light shine before others, so that they may see your good works and give glory to your Father in heaven."

When I speak with people who have become disenchanted with the Christian faith, I often find that their negative perception of Christianity stems from a bad experience with some pastor or churchgoer during a previous point in life. I have found this theme to be so prevalent that it's led me to often say, "If it weren't for Christians there'd be a lot more Christians."

Mahatma Gandhi is one of the most respected leaders of modern history. A Hindu, Gandhi nevertheless admired Jesus and often quoted from the Sermon on the Mount. E. Stanley Jones, a great Christian missionary and close friend of Gandhi, reportedly asked, "Mr. Gandhi, though you quote the words of Christ often, why is that you appear to so adamantly reject becoming his follower?" Gandhi replied, "Oh, I don't reject your Christ. I love your Christ. It's just that so many of you Christians are so unlike your Christ." I have heard that line quoted many times, but have yet to find a verified attestation to it. Whether or not Gandhi said those exact words, I cannot prove one way or the other, but we can be sure that Gandhi, at the least, thought very much along those lines. A record exists of Gandhi giving Jones some great advice when Jones asked how he might better reach people in India with the gospel. Gandhi's reply was as follows: "First, I would suggest that all of you Christians, missionaries and all, must begin to live more like Jesus Christ. Second, practice your religion without adulterating it or toning it down. Third, emphasize love and make it your working force, for love is central in Christianity. Fourth, study the non-Christian religions more sympathetically to find the good that is within them, in order to have a more sympathetic approach to the people."[1] Ghandi's words are so insightful, and so close to the heart of true Christianity, it makes me wonder how and why he never ended up as a Christian.

According to E. Stanley Jones's biography, Gandhi's rejection of Christianity grew out of an incident that happened when he was a young man practicing law in South Africa. He had become attracted to the Christian faith, had studied the Bible and the teachings of Jesus, and was seriously exploring becoming a Christian. And so he decided to attend a church service. As he came up the steps of the large church where he intended to go, a white South African elder of the church barred his way at the door. "Where do you think you're going, kaffir?" the man asked. Gandhi replied, "I'd like to attend worship here." The church elder snarled at him, "There's no room for kaffirs in this church. Get out of here or I'll have my assistants throw you down the steps." From that moment, Gandhi said, he decided to adopt what good he found in Christianity but would never again consider becoming a Christian if it meant being part of the church.

The example of Gandhi, unfortunately, is not uncommon. For one reason or another, people have been turned away from Christ by the very people claiming to serve him. I think we need to firmly fix in our mind the idea that we live "onstage." When we exit our church or home we are the physical connection to Christ for the world to view. When we follow the words of Christ, when we let our light shine, then we will see people attracted to Christ. When we allow our bad mood or self-centeredness to reflect something other than the light of Christ, we (often unknowingly) turn people away from the one they are seeking. Evangelism really is not that hard. People are naturally attracted to Christ. When we live out his teachings, letting our light shine, people will want to find out more. When we claim to follow Christ but reflect our own ways, people will walk away. It's that simple. We may not literally paint the exit door of our church or home blue like at Disney World, but every time you walk out that door, fix firmly in your mind that you are walking "onstage" so that your attitude and actions positively reflect upon the One we represent.

DO THE RIGHT THING, NOT THE EASY THING

As I was growing up, both of my parents impressed upon me constantly the idea that integrity means making the right choice when no one else is looking, or when it's the harder choice to make. I have tried to pass along that same bit of advice to my children. Renae and I remind Caleb and Cole almost daily what it means to make the right choice.

Life is made up of a collection of choices. When your alarm goes off in the morning you have to make a choice: Do you get out of bed or hit the snooze button? Choices continue throughout the day. What do you eat for lunch? In what order do you work through your to-do list? Do you show up for church on Wednesday night or do you stay late at the office trying to get one more thing finished? Do you make it to your child's soccer practice or hang out with your coworkers? Some choices are pretty easy. For instance, no one's life is going to be affected by which tie I choose to wear. Other decisions are extremely hard, such as whether you keep your date night with your spouse or stay late because your boss asked you to finish a project.

Part of living onstage means living a life of integrity. One of the big complaints I hear from non-Christians is that Christians are "a bunch of hypocrites." While I realize this is partially just an excuse, there is some truth to the matter. The word hypocrite comes from the Greek word *hypokrisis*, which means "play-acting." It's a reference to pretending to be something you're not or putting on a mask. It meant being an actor playing a role. In the case of Cast Members being onstage, they are playing roles. However, if they do not fully believe in what they are doing, you will quickly see through the sham. The same holds true for Christians. I am playing a role as a Christ-follower, but it goes way beyond just a role. My identity as a Christian is everything. It is the very core of my being. If I live my life any other way, those in the world around me will quickly see through the sham and turn away from Christ.

University of Alabama football coach Nick Saban gives an interesting challenge, "We are challenged daily to do the right things, and many times we fail. Cutting in front of someone in traffic because we're in a rush. Not returning a phone call because we don't want to deal with the issue at hand. Telling a coworker a white lie to cover our laziness. Skipping out on a son's baseball game because it's too hot outside. Sometime this week, take a day in your life to be mindful of this and make a mental note of how many times you have to make the right decision. . . . Many of us do the right thing most of the time, especially when the consequences for doing it are meaningless. Where we get tripped up is when doing the right thing can make us, or others, suffer."[2]

I took Saban's challenge seriously. I decided for an entire week to carry around a journal in an attempt to record how often I was forced to make the "right" decision, even minor decisions. I did not record decisions such as what to wear, but decisions where there was more of a clear-cut right or wrong response. Over the course of seven days, I made, on average, twenty-six "right/wrong" decisions each day. Some of them were major, affecting many people. Some of the decisions were minor. It's likely on those that no one other than me would have ever known. Those were the most difficult to choose correctly. I was astounded to see that my integrity was called into question that many times each day. At each one of those little "forks in the road" I had to remember who I am and whose I am. I challenge you to try this same activity. See how often you are forced to make decisions between right and wrong each day. How often do you do the right thing? When are you most tempted to not do the right thing?

There's an interesting story about a man who took a great risk to do the right thing. The supposedly true story begins in the office of Gordon Selfridge, the American-born retail mogul who founded the department store Selfridge's in England. Selfridge was having a conversation with one of his employees. The phone rings and Selfridge tells his employee, Gibbo, to answer it. When Selfridge hears who's on the other line he says to Gibbo, "Tell him I'm not here." Gibbo hands the phone to his boss and says, "You tell him." When Selfridge got off the phone he was furious. Gibbo said, "If I can lie for you, I can lie to you." He was the most trusted man in the company from that moment on. I don't know if this story is true or not. It was conveyed to me as true, but I can't back that up. The point of the story is applicable either way. This is an example of when doing the right thing was the most difficult thing. Would you have the guts to say something similar to your boss? Gibbo's actions proved him to be a man of integrity, even when it wasn't easy to be so.

Doing the right thing is always going to be most difficult when no one else is looking or when the "right" decision might bring negative consequences. For instance, if I mess up at work or church do I blame someone else, plead ignorance, or confess to my mistake? I'm sure the holy people reading this book will immediately say, "Confess!" But what if no one will ever know the difference? If I do the right thing and confess, I will suffer negative consequences. If I make one of the other two choices, no one will ever know and I get away clean. Do you see how difficult it is to make the right decision? The more serious the matter, the more difficult it is to choose correctly.

A common example is of driving while texting or talking on a cell phone. Recently, a couple of the cities around me passed ordinances making it illegal to use a cell phone or text while driving. These are considered a secondary violation, which means that you can't be given a ticket unless the police officer pulls you over for some other violation. Many people have commented to me that they'll never get caught so they'll keep right on texting and calling. This attitude demonstrates a lack of integrity. If you are only doing the right thing because you might be caught, you're not doing it for the right reason. Paul says in Romans 13:1, "Let every person be subject to the governing authorities; for there is no authority except from God, and those authorities that exist have been instituted by God." Christians are supposed to be good citizens, which means following the law of the land unless it specifically contradicts God's law. The people who choose to ignore these laws are doing it for selfish reasons. They don't want to be inconvenienced by not talking or texting on their phones for fifteen minutes, or however long it takes to get to their destination. They would rather break the law, and run the risk of causing an accident due to distracted driving, than do the right thing.

Living onstage means doing the right thing, all the time, because that's what being a Christ-follower means. I realize that sometimes we'll mess up and get it wrong. Praise God for God's mercy and grace in those situations! When we mess up, we confess and try to make the right decision next time. Whether you like it or not, people are watching you as a leader in the church. They want to see if you're a man or woman of integrity. Do you reflect the priorities of Jesus in your decision making? Do you put yourself or others first in making your decisions? Being a person of integrity is the first step in living onstage in a way that reflects Christ to the world.

I want to be sure that I'm clear on my definition of integrity. I'm not suggesting that you act one way in your home and then when you step outside you change into "onstage" mode. That would be the true definition of hypocrite—acting. I have debated with some of my Christian friends whether using profanity is okay. One of them has stated to me, "It's just words. And why should I pretend not to say those words in public if I say them in private?" His argument is one of authenticity. For him, and I agree with this, true integrity is being the same no matter where you are. However, I lean heavily on the Apostle Paul's wisdom in this discussion.

In 1 Corinthians 8, Paul discusses eating meat that has been offered to idols. Essentially, Paul says that eating meat offered to idols is no big deal for him because he knows that those other "gods" are not real. For him, meat is meat, regardless of where it came from. However, there were many new Christians who had not completely broken free of the old ways of thinking. They struggled with the idea of eating meat offered to idols. Paul's advice, then, is if your actions hurt someone else, don't do it. Specifically, he says in 1 Corinthians 8:12–13, "But when you thus sin against members of your family, and wound their conscience when it is weak, you sin against Christ. Therefore, if food is a cause of their falling, I will never eat meat, so that I may not cause one of them to fall." In other words, if eating that meat (or saying a cuss word) causes someone else to struggle, then I am guilty of sin.

Let me put it this way: I, personally, have no problem with the idea of a Christian drinking alcohol (drunkenness I have a very big problem with, but that's a different issue). If a fellow Christian wants to have a beer or glass of wine with supper, it's no big deal for me. I don't personally like the taste of alcohol, but I'm not offended if someone else does or if they drink in front of me. I also know, however, that there are some for whom this is a real problem, whether from the way they have been taught or from previous struggles. I would never go into a bar because I know that for some it would hurt my credibility as a Christian and as a pastor.

Paul says the folks who have a problem with eating meat offered to idols are "weak," and even though he disagrees with them, he still refuses to do it because he doesn't want to be a stumbling block for someone else. I do not want to imply that those who think drinking alcohol is a sin are "weak." I am saying that I recognize that Christians disagree on this issue and that, because alcohol is a stumbling block for some, I choose to distance myself from it.

Another example is that of gambling. I know several Christians who visit casinos while on vacation and see no problem with doing so. And I understand that. I could walk into a casino, spend $20, and walk out again with no lasting harm. However, I can't do that for two reasons. First, I'm a bad loser, and losing that $20 would probably do harm to my own spiritual journey. Second, casinos make a living preying, not on vacationers, but upon those who can least afford to lose that money. The argument I generally hear is, "That's their choice. No one is forcing them to go into the casino. Why should I stop because they make bad choices?" This is very reminiscent of Cain's famous question: "Am I my brother's keeper?" (Gen. 4:9). The answer in that situation, and in this one, is "Yes!" Maybe it doesn't hurt me, but it hurts someone else and, therefore, I lay aside my personal petty wants for the sake of others.

In the Disney system, being "onstage" means you put the guest ahead of yourself. Does the fact that I don't have a problem with someone having a beer, or going to a casino, yet I won't do it myself make me inauthentic? No. It means I'm putting others ahead of myself. I'm not offended by profanity, but I won't personally use it, again, because I know it would cause others to struggle. Paul says in 1 Corinthians 10:23, "'All things are lawful,' but not all things are beneficial. 'All things are lawful,' but not all things build up. Do not seek your own advantage, but that of the other." Part of the Christian life is denying self for the sake of others. Our American culture teaches that every individual is responsible for his or her own choices, but the Way of Jesus teaches that we are our brother's or sister's keeper and we are responsible for making sure they don't fall.

Authentic integrity, then, is always looking out for the best interests of others. It does not mean I act however I want, as long as I act the same at home and in public. When we choose to follow Christ we give up the right to do whatever we want. Instead, like Paul, we become concerned enough about the spiritual growth and well-being of others that we lay aside our own desires. Living onstage means that you live in a way that shows people the love of Christ, not that you show whatever you want.

CHARACTER MATTERS

Does character really matter that much for a Christian leader? Absolutely! Character is becoming more and more an issue in the political arena. It's also vitally important in the business world. I was fascinated that Jim Collins found that the character of the CEO played a large role in whether a company made the jump from good to great. Further, Collins writes, "In determining the 'right people,' the good-to-great companies placed greater weight on character attributes than on specific educational background, practical skills, specialized knowledge, or work experience. Not that specific knowledge or skills are unimportant, but they viewed these traits as more teachable (or at least learnable), whereas they believed dimensions like character, work ethic, basic intelligence, dedication to ful-filling commitments, and values are more ingrained."[3]

Collins's research shows an important reality for Christians—others care about our character. Guys like Jim Baker and Jimmy Swaggert, along with the recent scandals in the Catholic Church, have helped reduce the perceived integrity of Christian clergy, especially, to almost nothing in our culture. Pastors used to be universally respected, regardless of a person's faith. This is no longer the case. Christians, in general, are no longer necessarily viewed as "good." The character of our leaders is more important than ever.

I agree almost completely with Collins's assessment. When you are looking for new leaders within your church, a commitment to Christ and the highest character must be a top priority. It does not matter how tal-ented a person is, if he or she is not spiritually mature that individual will end up being a hindrance to your mission. Where I disagree with Collins is that character is ingrained. I think we have a basic inclination towards doing the right thing or not, but Christian character and maturity is not ingrained. It is grown within us by the Holy Spirit. Thus, if a person does not have an active relationship with Jesus, that person will not possess the character necessary to accomplish the mission of God.

As Christians, we cannot be "volunteers." A volunteer is someone who simply gives some time or resources to help others. For a Christian leader, following Christ must be a way of life, not just something we do occasionally. This is what I suggest you look for when looking for new leaders to mentor and raise up within your church. Thus, discipleship training truly becomes leadership training. As persons become more devoted disciples of Christ, they simultaneously become more fit to be leaders within the community of faith.

Lee Cockerell states that Disney specifically trains leaders in character, not just skills.[4] I have seen this in action. I left something in our hotel room. Mousekeeping (the term for the cleaning crew) found it in my hotel room. They could have kept it or thrown it away. Instead, I received a package in the mail containing my lost item. I've seen Cast Members search tirelessly to help a child find a lost toy or a distraught lady find her purse. I specifically remember being on the Big Thunder Mountain Railroad ride with my oldest son, Caleb. As we pulled back into the station we saw a young girl standing next to a Cast Member. The Cast Member informed us that the little girl had lost her teddy bear and asked if we would please look for it. We all searched our seats, and someone found the bear stuffed into one of the bag holders. Obviously, a joyful reunion ensued and the Cast Member had just created a magical memory for that little girl. But she didn't have to do that. She could have done as I've seen employees at other theme parks do: "Sorry. If we find it, we'll send it to lost and found." But because Disney trains for character, this Cast Member went the extra mile to help a guest in need.

The kind of character we are talking about is not inherent. I mentioned that the Holy Spirit grows this character within us, but it also has to be passed on from mentor to student. As a leader, you are a role model. Your job is to reproduce the Christian character DNA within you in the next generation of leaders. As you do the right thing and model character, the next generation will pick up that DNA. They will understand what's most important by what you model and how you treat them.

Character won't develop overnight, but keep encouraging those around you to become what God created them to be. As Johann Wolfgang von Goethe, the famous German writer and philosopher said, "Treat people as if they were what they ought to be and you help them become what they are capable of becoming."[5] Let those around you see what Christian character looks like as you live onstage for Christ and they will begin to emulate what they see.

R-E-S-P-E-C-T

Another aspect of living onstage is showing respect to all those around you, whether you like them or agree with them or not. Jesus had an incredible ability to show love and respect to all people, even those hurling insults at him. From the cross he asked for forgiveness for those who had treated him so harshly (Luke 23:34). We are to show the same respect and love to all persons. Whether we like them or not, God loves them and died for them. That makes them worthy of our respect, regardless of how they act.

Disney trains its Cast Members to show respect to all persons. They have to be able to respect people of all backgrounds. Guests come from every country, race, religious background, and socioeconomic status. They also deal with people of both genders and all sexual orientations. If Cast Members can't be respectful to people of all types, they are in trouble because whoever they have a problem with will definitely be at the parks. Disney knows that treating every guest with respect results in good will toward the company and increases the bottom line. Therefore, every Cast Member is drilled in respect.

Respect is vital. It does not mean accepting every belief. You can be respectful while still disagreeing. During one of my Wednesday night Bible studies at RSUMC, someone asked if I would bow my head during a prayer to another god. For instance, if I were invited to an interfaith prayer breakfast, would I bow my head when a Muslim or Hindu prayed? The answer is no. But I would remain still and silent out of respect. I won't bow my head to anyone but God, but that doesn't mean I have to make a spectacle of myself, either. I remain silent during the national anthems of countries other than my own and I don't mind hearing someone of another religion pray. My hope is that by showing them respect, I might gain their attention and they would, in turn, respectfully hear the case for Christ. So, while I don't endorse or agree with every belief out there, I can still be respectful toward every person.

When I, as a Christian leader, disrespect other beliefs or culture, I lose my ability to have an audience with those I'm trying to reach. If I spend all of my time condemning Muslims do you think they'll be willing to listen to what I have to say? In the United Methodist Church, like other denominations, there has been strong disagreement among the members regarding the place of homosexuality in the Christian faith, specifically among the ranks of ordained clergy. If either side spends all of its time condemning rather than listening, will anything be accomplished? For that matter, if I focus on condemning others regarding any issue where that person might believe differently than me, will he or she be willing to give my viewpoint an audience? No. To get respect, you have to first give respect. I think one of the things that has most damaged the church's witness in the world is the way in which a few outspoken intolerant people have represented Christ. Now much of the rest of the world believes those few represent the majority of Christians. We prove those to be the minority by showing the love of Christ and due respect to all people. However, being a Christian leader means giving respect without having to have it in return. Jesus never demanded that people believe any certain way before he loved them. Neither should we.

ROLE PLAY

One of the best ways to develop your character, and that of others, is to role play. Sit down with your ministry team, your small group, your pastor, or whomever you trust and brainstorm every ethical dilemma you might encounter in your role as a Christian leader—not just at church, but also in your everyday life. Most of living onstage happens outside the walls of the church building. Therefore, you need to practice your responses for work, family, and friends before they occur in reality.

Ethical dilemmas can present themselves in a variety of ways. If you know a fellow leader in the church is involved in an adulterous affair, do you keep your mouth shut or do you say something? If you decide to talk, to whom do you speak? If your boss asks you to fudge the numbers a little to make him look good, what do you do? What if you see someone take some money out of the offering plate, but you also know that person's family is in extreme financial need?

I have found that most of the time, when brainstorming ethical dilemmas, most people look at the situations before them and say, "I have no idea what I'd do." Right! And you won't in reality either. Most people, when presented with such difficult situations, simply freeze. It's not that they don't want to do the right thing, but that they don't know what to do and so end up doing nothing. By spending time role playing ethical situations you can train yourself to respond in the appropriate manner.

I'M WATCHING YOU

One of the catch phrases from the movie *Meet the Parents* is "I'm watching you." Robert Di Niro's character, the father of the bride, is a former CIA operative who is constantly spying on Ben Stiller's character to see if he is "worthy" of his daughter.[6] While this phrase makes for humor and conflict between the characters, it's also a good one for us to remember as we go onstage.

There have been numerous occasions where my children have said or done something that I'm not too happy about. I immediately turn to my wife and say, "Where did they learn that?" How do you think she responds? "From you." It's amazing how much our kids absorb just from being around us. They watch our every move. I'm amazed to sometimes hear very profound things come out of the mouths of my boys. They overhear a conversation between me and Renae and process what they hear. Sometimes I think they're not paying attention during worship, and then during lunch Caleb will ask me a very deep question. I've learned my kids are constantly observing.

The world around us is much the same. They are watching you when you claim to be a Christian. They want to see if this God-thing makes any difference. Why should they give up their Sunday morning golf game to go to church if you act just like they do? The answer is: they shouldn't. They need to see God at work in your life before they are willing to listen to what you have to say.

I have heard countless sermons quoting St. Francis of Assisi as saying, "Preach the gospel at all times. Use words when necessary." After doing a good bit of research I discovered he never actually said that. I did discover that, "In Chapter XVII of his Rule of 1221, Francis told the friars not to preach unless they had received the proper permission to do so. Then he added, 'Let all the brothers, however, preach by their deeds.'"[7] The concept is similar in both the quote we know Assisi made and the one often attributed to him. Our actions speak as loudly as, or louder than, our words. I have heard that quote used as an excuse to avoid sharing one's faith. I don't buy that as an excuse. We are certainly called to share our faith, but if we don't live our faith as well, then our words are meaningless.

How likely is someone to listen to me if that person sees me berating my young son at his football game on Saturday and then hears me talking about mercy and grace on Sunday? How likely will someone be to listen if I preach about loving all and then laugh at a sexist or racist joke? Yes, words are important, but those words must be backed up by action. In social constructionist thought, words actually are action. Words are never used in a vacuum. They also perform some function within a relationship. Either they build trust by being demonstrated through action, or they tear at the fabric of the relationship when actions contradict the words. So words become an integrity issue. Do the words spoken match the actions taken?

It is in this last sentence that I find some of my highest respect for Disney. All of their corporate values and mission sound good, but they have to live them out on a daily basis. They can talk about respect and putting the guest first, but if they don't live it "onstage," everyone will know in a hurry that all of their talk is just that. Several thousand people are examining Disney's training, ethics, and core values on a daily basis. Do they live them out with integrity? My experience has been, overall, yes. That's why people keep coming back.

Whether you have fifty people or five thousand in your church on a weekend, people are looking to see if your talk matches your actions. Your training is meaningless if you don't model the desired behavior. People will care about your words only if they see them in action. A picture may be worth a thousand words, but words lived out through action "onstage" are invaluable.

PROPER BOUNDARIES

A final aspect of living onstage is your ability to demonstrate proper boundaries. If you are to be a person of integrity, you have to know when to say, "No." When you see an ethical situation arising, do you have the courage to walk away from the situation? Can you say no to your peers if they try to persuade you to do something that you know might damage your integrity?

When I talk about damaging your integrity, I'm not just talking about your reputation with your coworkers. I'm talking about the living out of your core values. If you say God is your top priority and family is second, do your actions reflect that? Do you leave work in time to get to your kids' soccer practice? Do you say no to extra work to take that date night? Do you honor your commitments to God in your family and in your church, or do you allow others to pressure you into violating those boundaries?

Living onstage means everyone is looking. You put others first. And that also means you have to draw the line in the sand firmly and not cross it. I make a habit of putting Caleb's football practice and Cole's soccer practice in my planner just like any other appointment. If someone tries to schedule a meeting during that time I say, "Sorry. I already have a meeting planned."

I stay extremely busy, as I'm sure you do. Life's pressures seem nonstop. If I don't set firm boundaries, it's possible I will violate what I say I most believe in before I realize what's happening. Living onstage doesn't mean you say yes to everything that comes your way. Know when to say no and you'll be more effective when you say yes.

CONCLUSION

I enjoy being involved in community theater. In a recent production I directed, one of the characters says, "That's what I hate about stages—there's no place to hide!"[8] That statement is true of us as Christians. Once we walk through our metaphorical, or literal, blue doors and go "onstage," there's no place to hide. The world sees us as we are, and we want to come across as genuine, not phony, in our desire to live God's life.

We need to constantly remind ourselves that we live in the world representing God, not living for ourselves. I've seen several churches that have "You are now entering the mission field" over their exit doors. I like that, but I heard Erwin McManus once comment that Christianity is not about following rules but about unleashing a life more incredible than anything we could dream possible on our own.[9] When we step "onstage" we are not doing so to "do" anything to anyone else or to make them like us. We are doing it to help them become like Christ. We are doing it to model what this incredible life looks like, to serve as an example to others, and to lead them to the One who can help them to experience the same incredible life.

★

LIVING INTO THE LESSON

1. What is your reaction to being "onstage" for Christ? How can you use this concept in your ministry and life?

2. The author states that "every time you walk out that door, fix firmly in your mind that you are walking 'onstage' so that your attitude and actions positively reflect upon the One we represent." How can this change transform your life and the lives of others? What can you do to bring to mind this concept while you are "onstage"?

3. How do you make your "integrity" decisions each day? How can you be more intentional about choosing the right way?

4. How does putting aside your own desires to look out for the needs of others make you a better leader? In what areas do you need to commit to putting this into practice?

5. In what areas are you most comfortable modeling Christian character for those you are mentoring? In what areas do you need to be a better model?

6. How can role play make you more equipped to handle ethical difficulties you may encounter?

7. How well do your actions match your talk? In what areas do you need to show more integrity in your words and action?

8. How well defined are your boundaries? Where do you need to make changes to become more filled with integrity?

EIGHT ★ BRINGING THE MAGIC HOME

If you can dream it, you can do it.

—WALT DISNEY

Obviously, my family can't live at Walt Disney World, though I'm fairly certain my boys would if they could find a way. However, we try to find ways to keep Disney at home with us. We have lots of videos, all of our vacation pictures, CDs of the theme park music, and both our kitchen and master bathroom are Disney themed. We are constantly looking for ways to experience the Disney magic while we're not at the parks. We want to bring a bit of the magic home with us.

I hope, after reading the previous chapters, that you want to bring the magic home, too. You may be wondering where to begin. After the first visit to a Disney park, most people walk away with their head spinning. It's almost impossible to conceptualize just how much there is to do until you actually experience it. So it is in this case. After the first read-through you might have a million ideas racing through your head, but no idea where to begin. The purpose of this chapter is to help you put some of the principles you've read about into practice.

I have to begin by being completely honest. Implementing the principles outlined in these pages won't be easy. Disney Cast Member and author Alice Bass writes, "Being available to creativity is not as easy as it looks on paper. You already know because you have risked before. You handed in your drawing and it was the only one that the teacher did not put up on the board. You set aside time to write the story brewing in your head, only to cancel your personal time for a child who felt too sick to go to school. You came up with a great idea, but everyone around the conference table stared blankly until someone said, 'I don't get it.'"[1] Alice goes on to say that human beings were created by God to be creative, yet we often fall short of that gift because of our fear of rejection.

You are going to face the same fear of rejection when you bring up any new idea. People, by nature, are fairly resistant to change, and that attitude appears to be magnified when someone steps through the doors of a church building. Your first step in doing anything great for God is overcoming your fear. When Caleb was younger he was almost afraid of his own shadow. We tried to plug him into soccer and he broke down in tears every practice. We tried to get him to do swimming lessons and he cried nonstop before every time in the pool. On his first night of taekwondo classes Caleb cried and begged me not to make him do it. Each time I tried to remind Caleb that it's okay to be afraid of trying something new as long as we never let our fear stop us. At ten years old, Caleb is now a second-degree black-belt, a certified scuba diver, and a football player. He still feels nervous before any new experience, but he no longer allows that fear to overcome him, and I'm very proud of him for that.

I'm giving the same advice to you. It's okay to be afraid of failure, or afraid to try something new. Just don't let that fear stop you from trying. You'll never accomplish anything big for God (remember the BHAG from chapter 3?) if you don't address your fears first. Wayne Gretzky, arguably the greatest hockey player of all time, once said, "You miss 100% of the shots you don't take."[2] Yes, you might fail. But you definitely will fail if you never try.

You also need to address the tendency toward having a fatalistic attitude. I have seen this attitude creep up in church leaders time and again. They go to conferences or read a new book and come back with a plethora of new ideas that are promptly shot down by the establishment. I have had some of these leaders say, in essence, "Our church hasn't had a new idea since the Great Revival and still sings out of the Cokesbury hymnal, even though they are all falling apart because they are so old. I want to try something new, but I know I'll never be allowed to implement any idea I present." If they don't give up altogether, they keep bringing the ideas but eventually present them with the attitude of, "I know you're going to say no, but here it is anyway."

Your enthusiasm will carry a lot of weight in selling new ideas. Some people are going to say no regardless of how good the idea is. Just expect that and move on. If you wait for 100 percent approval you'll rarely accomplish anything. Find those who will buy into the new idea and proceed with them. Those people might be just a small minority, or they might be the overwhelming majority. Either way, find out who is willing to walk with you on this journey and get moving instead of feeling stuck because a few (or one or two) say no.

Just because you are enthusiastic, however, does not mean that you will accomplish your mission. Many politicians are fantastic orators. They give great campaign speeches and pep talks and yet never accomplish anything in office. Don't you become like them. As Bill Hybels says, "There's a huge difference between visionary leadership and getting-it-done leadership" (or git-r-done leadership, as we might say in my area).[3] Many leaders are good cheerleaders. Others are faithful in repeating the vision over and over. Both of those things are good, but they don't accomplish anything. So, let's start talking about how to get something accomplished.

SHARE THE WEALTH

If you like the ideas found within this book, step one is to share those ideas with others. You can't begin a discussion with anyone unless you're all approaching the discussion from the same frame of reference. If you sit down with others in your church and start talking about Blue Sky thinking, being an EPCOT Church, and living onstage, they will look at you like you've begun speaking in tongues. And, in essence, you have started thinking and speaking in an "unknown" language. So the first step is to encourage whatever group you have influence over to read this book and begin a study together. Use the Living into the Lesson questions at the end of every chapter to foster your discussion. Make the group about nothing other than exploring a new framework for approaching church leadership. You won't attempt to change anything or start any new ministries at first. Just read the book and see what thoughts it sparks in others.

During 2010, I participated in an "incubator" group with several other clergy and lay people from within my conference. (In the United Methodist system, the conference is all of the churches in a geographic area overseen by one bishop. In my case, that means all the United Methodist churches in Alabama south of Birmingham and including the Florida panhandle.) The group was run by a facilitator from Spiritual Leadership, Inc., which is an organization that specializes in helping churches and denominational hierarchy come together in a think-tank environment.[4] Throughout the first half of the incubator group we prayed together, shared our lives, and studied specific topics. The study included teachings by our facilitator as well as reading and discussing specific books. By the end of the first half we were all speaking a similar language and had built a common framework. From that point on, we were able to dream and plan together.

It doesn't matter how many people you ask to join this group. If you have too many, form more than one group. The point is that discussion will begin. When discussions begin, dreams begin. As people are exposed to new ideas, they will begin making application of those ideas to their own setting. You'll feel that Disney magic running rampant in your board meetings as people connect what they read with their unique situation.

Part of the discussion should also include more than this book. This book is not the only, nor the best, book on leadership. I have, hopefully, added something to the leadership discussion by giving you some new ways to think about Christian leadership, but there are plenty of other books that will give you other perspectives. If you don't know where to start, just go through those listed in the Notes section. That's certainly not an all-inclusive list, but it at least gives you a starting point. Each of those books will have its own bibliography from which you can gain knowledge of even more resources.

Once everyone has the same point of reference, then you're ready to start doing something with your knowledge. If you read the book, discuss it, then put it on the shelf to gather dust, you've wasted your time. Remember, Walt's mantra was "dream, believe, dare, do." The "do" is the most important part. So, let's get ready to take the next step.

HOW TO EAT AN ELEPHANT

I love the joke that asks, "How do you eat an elephant?" The answer, "One bite at a time." If you're in a church that hasn't made any major changes in many years, trying to implement these concepts will seem like trying to eat an elephant. So don't focus on all of the changes that need to be made. Take things one bite at a time.

You've laid the foundation by studying and praying together as a group. The next step is to hold Blue Sky sessions to come up with all of the ways your ministry or church needs to change. The list might contain a few ideas or you might fill up an entire notebook. It depends on how expansive an area you're trying to cover. Obviously, if you're trying to implement changes across an entire church, your list will be much larger than someone dealing with a specific ministry. Either way, make your list and then prioritize each item on the list.

You can prioritize your list anyway you wish, but I'll share with you my method. I started using the Franklin Planner system many years ago. On my "to-do" list for each day I was to write beside each item an A, B, or C. A meant that the item was vital and I needed to take care of it immediately. I usually only have one or two of those on my list each day. B meant that the item was important but could wait, and C meant that the item was not important; I could get to it whenever I had a free moment.[5] That's a fairly simple and easy way to break everything down.

Lately, I've begun using the method espoused by Stephen Covey.[6] This method places tasks or issues into one of four quadrants. Quadrant 1 (Q1) means something is both important and urgent. You would put something in this category that is a pressing problem that is preventing you from succeeding in ministry or a crisis of some sort. For instance, when I began at RSUMC the children's program consisted of my two boys. Then, over a fairly short period of time, we found ourselves inundated with new families with young children. Suddenly we had lots of kids, but no ministry for them. We had to deal with the situation immediately. That concern was both important (kids are a priority for us) and urgent.

A Quadrant 2 (Q2) issue is something that is important, but not urgent. Right now at RSUMC we have grown to the point where our sanctuary is comfortably full. We recognize the need to start a second service. We also want to offer a different style of worship. So a new worship service is an issue that, for us, is important, but it's not urgent. The church isn't going to fall apart if we don't get it done in the next couple of weeks.

A Quadrant 3 (Q3) task would be something not important, but urgent. This is stuff you have to do, but wouldn't be considered vital to the effectiveness of your ministry. For instance, the United Methodist polity requires that our Church Council meet at least quarterly. There's not always anything terribly important that we have to discuss at these meetings, but we do have to deal with these meetings in a timely manner, which places it under the "urgent" status.

The final quadrant is Quadrant 4 (Q4), which is for those items neither important nor urgent. Something that falls under this category might be planning a church picnic. It's not "important" in that your ministry is not going to be terribly impacted one way or the other by it. It's not "urgent" because you can do that pretty much any time of the year. It's still a good thing to do so you keep it on your list. Because of my extremely limited time and hectic schedule, most things that I designate Q4 I simply eliminate. If it's not urgent or important, I really don't have time for it. That's not to say all Q4 items should be eliminated, but if you have to choose things to drop completely, this would be the quadrant to use to scale down your list.

Let me make the difference in terms very clear. Urgent refers to something that has to be acted upon immediately. Important is something that furthers our vision and mission. If it doesn't further our mission and vision, it might be good, but it's not important. If it doesn't require immediate action, even if we want it badly, it's not urgent. Also, realize that something might not fall under "important" for your ministry team, but it might be very important to another team. You'll have to learn to work within the framework of other teams to create a successful overall church.

Go through your Blue Sky list and designate every item Q1, Q2, Q3, or Q4. Or use the A, B, C method, or whatever other method you choose. The key is that you categorize your "to-do" list. By working through your list you will see which "bite" you need to take first. Sometimes the things you want to work on the most are not the things that demand your attention. Sometimes you have to work in steps: in order to accomplish Goal A, I first have to work through Tasks B and C.

Once everything on your list has a priority, go over it again. If you have ten things in Q1, you've either gone overboard or you need to delegate. I try to make sure that I never have more than three things on my Q1 list at any one time. If I see more than three, I call in reinforcements and delegate what I can. Sometimes I look back at the list and realize I had defined something as urgent but, in actuality, it could wait a week or two.

Now, by asking you to create these quadrants, I have made the assumption that there is an existing mission and vision statement for your team and/or church. If not, you need to start there. Without a vision, you can't designate what's important and what's not. Creating a mission/vision statement is something that often takes a long time in a church (way too long, in my opinion). So create one for you personally, or for your team, that can define what you're about. Once the church, as a whole, has a mission and vision statement in place, then you can adjust your team's statement to fall in line with the overall mission of the church. If you choose the Great Commandment (love God with all of your being and your neighbor as yourself) and the Great Commission (make disciples) as your mission statement, you won't go wrong, no matter in which arena you're serving.

I realize that only giving a paragraph or two to creating a mission or vision statement hardly seems adequate. However, that's not the purpose of this book. If you need help in creating a mission or vision statement, there are numerous excellent resources.[7] Let me just say that I define a mission statement as being a quick, easy-to-remember statement that sums up the core of what your church or ministry is all about. This rarely changes. Disney's mission of making people happy has varied slightly in the wording over the years, but the basic message is exactly the same. The vision statement is a description with specific steps of how you will accomplish that mission. The vision statement can be updated on a regular basis. Some sources define vision as what life will look like if you live out your mission, and strategies are thought of as the steps toward how to fulfill that mission and vision. However you want to define those steps is fine. Just make sure you work through those ideas and have a clear direction of where you are going.

No matter what you choose, you must let your mission and vision define what is important and what is not. Without the mission and vision to direct that "this is what we're all about," making a statement about importance is pure opinion. Obviously, if the mission of your current church is to keep things absolutely the same until everyone dies or Jesus comes back, then you have a problem if you want to be an EPCOT church leader. I make that statement only slightly with tongue in cheek. I see churches every day that want to be left alone. They have no desire to reach anyone new or to do anything different. If you're in one of these churches, then you have two choices: fight or leave. What you cannot do is give up. If God has sparked something within you through the pages of this book, if you feel a burning desire to make a difference for God's realm, then you can't simply say, "Oh, well" and go back to business as usual.

If you're feeling discouraged, go read Ezekiel 37. God brings life back to dry bones. That vision was God's way of showing Ezekiel that there is nothing beyond God's power to bring back to life. No church and person is so far gone that they could never experience God's resurrection. So, if you're in the deadest, driest, dustiest old church imaginable, there is hope! Catch God's vision, be faithful to what God tells you, and watch the resurrection happen.

If, as ancient Israel often did, the people of your church refuse to catch the vision, then possibly its time for you to look elsewhere. God never forces people to change, and you can't either. If they're not interested, then take your passion to a place where God can use you. I realize that if you are part of the family in a "family" church, this can be an extremely difficult decision. Those types of churches are often the most resistant to change, and the most in need of the change. At this point, you are faced with loyalty to God's calling or loyalty to your blood family. Do you stick it out and try to change things in a place very unlikely to change, or do you risk the wrath of your family in order to pursue God's call? For me, God's call takes precedent over everything, but you have to make that decision for yourself.

I am not a fan at all of church hopping, and I am deeply disgusted by the consumerist attitude our current culture takes toward church (meet my needs or I'll just shop around for another church), but I am also a realist. You can only fight for so long before you realize you're wasting your time. I cannot tell you how long that fight will last. That has to be a decision between you and God. Just know that no church, or person, is beyond redemption and change if they're willing.

BABY STEPS

If you've made it this far, you've made some real progress! So far you have a mission and vision, and you've identified the tasks before you, those things you need to do and those that you dream of doing. You've determined, in some manner, how urgent and important each of those tasks is based upon how they relate to the vision and the mission. You can use whichever categorization process you wish, but I'm going to use the Quadrant style I mentioned above for the purpose of examples.

The next step is to decide which of the Q3 items you have to deal with, and then delegate someone to deal with those or deal with them as a team using minimal effort and resources. Remember, those things are unimportant, but they are urgent, so you can't ignore them. Then, choose which of your Q1 items deserves the most attention. If you have more than one item in your first quadrant, then you must prioritize those, or delegate one or more to another team. Sometimes a ministry item can fit Q1 for multiple teams, so delegate if possible. Q2 items are your "dream" items. RSUMC wants to build a new family life center. We've grown to the point where we need more space, but it's not urgent. This is a dream, but letting it go for several months, or even a year or two, won't greatly reduce our ability to do ministry. Eventually it will enhance our ministry, so it's definitely important, but it's not urgent.

Whatever your main Q1 issue is, start by discussing what needs to happen in order to accomplish your goal. I would recommend choosing the Q1 issue first that will be the easiest victory. Many of us want to tackle the most difficult issues first. However, those issues possess the greatest risk and potential for your becoming bogged down. When you're first starting to introduce a new way of thinking you need momentum. Momentum comes from quick victories. So pick something with few to no obstacles that almost everyone will agree on. Success breeds success. Accomplishing the easy victories gives confidence, hope, and energy to tackle the really important and difficult tasks later on.

As we were getting on track at RSUMC, getting everyone behind a children's ministry provided a quick victory and a lot of momentum. Beyond a few folks who were willing to commit to the ministry, we didn't need a lot of resources to make that happen. Everyone agreed it was important and supported it. In the end, getting that children's ministry going got the entire church excited and provided momentum for growth. Once you gain momentum, then tackle the tougher Q1 issues.

REALITY CHECK

You can't accomplish your new goal without knowing what it will take and how you are positioned at present to deal with the issues ahead. I love my GPS device, but before that little computer can tell me where to go, it first has to acquire the satellite signal so that it will know where it is currently located. You can't figure out the map to where you want to go unless you know your starting point. Many people are willing to dream about the future, but a big obstacle in acting upon that dream is not knowing where to begin.

In order to figure out where you are, take a look at your dream and ask if resistance exists in making this dream a reality. If so, what shifts in structure or attitude need to take place to overcome that resistance? Are there any other churches or resources in the area trying to accomplish the same ministry? If so, is there a way to partner with them or should you attempt another ministry rather than duplicating what already exists? For instance, if you're trying to overcome poverty in your community, there is plenty of work for everyone. Find out what other ministries and organizations are working toward this goal, and see how your ministry can plug in with them. If you're looking at doing a new type of worship service, partnering with other churches may not be feasible. You still need to look around and find out what everyone else is doing. If every church in the area is doing "contemporary" worship, do you really need to do that style of worship too? Can you find something else to make your ministry unique?

The next step in assessing your present reality is to create an inventory of the resources, including people power, financial backing, and facility requirements, that you will need to accomplish the task. At least then you'll know the size of the mountain you're trying to climb. You may look at the mountain and decide, right now, you're ill-equipped to climb it. It takes a much different set of resources to climb Mount Everest than it does to go rock climbing in your local nature preserve. If you see that the resource requirements are out of your reach, then move that Q1 item to Q2. This is your reality check. It might seem urgent to you at this moment that you get that new ministry started, but if you don't have the resources to accomplish it, you'll need to find another solution to address the problem.

If you examine your resources and determine you have what is required, the next step is to determine the obstacles. Often we only think of obstacles in terms of available resources (financial, people needed, and facility), but you've already addressed that issue. The obstacles I'm talking about may be less obvious. These may be power cliques within the church that want to control every ministry or a low self-esteem within a church that doesn't believe it can ever make a difference. Certainly you'll encounter a fear of taking risks anytime you try something new.

Whatever obstacles you face, diagnose which ones are most critical for you to circumvent in order to be successful. Some obstacles you'll never remove. As I mentioned, some people are going to be stubborn and resist change even if Jesus personally walks into the church and suggests the idea. Other obstacles, though, are possible to overcome. Indeed, some of them are essential to overcome in order to achieve success. All obstacles should be confronted scripturally, openly, with love, and courageously. Don't run over anyone. Don't bankrupt the church while trying to achieve your goals. But don't shy away either.

Some obstacles will require that you adapt your goal. Boxer Mike Tyson once said, "Everybody has a plan until they get punched in the face."[8] You will encounter frustrations and failures any time you're trying to do something great for God. Expect it and adapt. It's fascinating for me to talk to the Disney Imagineers and hear what the original concepts were for many of their attractions and how those attractions evolved and become better because of adversity and conflict. The Imagineers have built a culture of embracing positive conflict, not running from it. Every Imagineer I spoke with agreed that conflict is what helps make a good idea into a great idea. Approach conflict with the same attitude and you'll soon discover it's a new tool, not something to be feared.

When I say positive conflict, I am referring to the creative tension that occurs when people start sharing ideas. In this environment, no one takes criticism personally and no criticism is presented as a personal attack. All ideas are valued and given due consideration, no matter how outrageous those ideas may seem. When everyone is passionate about a goal, conflict will naturally happen. However, if everyone is working toward the same goal and everyone genuinely cares about those around them, then conflict will result in an even stronger idea and better team.

Our cultural narrative is that conflict is bad and we should avoid it at all costs. That usually results in a lame-duck, watered-down ministry. Conflict is like fire. It can be used for good or for destruction. When the narrative is rewritten and conflict becomes seen as a positive, your team will grow closer together. The only way to rewrite that narrative is to create an environment of complete safety and acceptance. That takes time, but it can be done.

GO!

Walt Disney said, "The way to get started is to quit talking and begin doing."[9] Eventually you have to quit the planning and put the plan into action. Giving the green light to your plan means risking failure, but you need to embrace that potential failure. The Imagineers, also, have embraced failure as part of the learning curve. So quit worrying and jump in! I appreciate the statement by the great philosopher, Yoda: "Do or do not. There is no try."[10] That needs to be your attitude, too. Go for it, 100 percent. If you fail, learn from that failure and go again. The greatest Blue Sky ideas in the world are worthless until put into action.

How you implement can be one of the most important parts of your planning. Make sure that you have everything ready and that you launch your idea at the most advantageous time. For instance, most churches experience a bit of a lull during the summer. That would probably not be the best time to launch a new idea. Or, in your context, maybe it is. But give timing some thought. Also, be sure you get as many people excited and on board before you launch, even if they have nothing to do with the actual implementation. We all need cheerleaders, and word of mouth is the best way to get free advertising for your new idea.

Once you launch, there are two key components. First is transparency. Make sure the entire process is documented so that you can go back later and see where you went right and where you might have made mistakes. Also, should anyone want to know why you made certain choices, you should be able to show them the process. Full transparency is the key to maintaining your integrity and making sure your opponents have no foothold against you.

The second key is to celebrate. You need to celebrate every milestone and every effort by those on your team. Celebrations keep the momentum going. Celebrate both publicly and privately, as a team. Reward those on your team who put forth great effort and encourage others to do the same. In 2009, Disney began a promotion at its parks called "What will you celebrate?" The idea was to encourage every guest coming to Disney to celebrate something. They had birthday buttons, anniversary buttons, and also "I'm celebrating" buttons. The latter could be given for anything. Disney wanted guests to feel like every trip to their parks was a celebration. Ask your team, "What will we celebrate?" Find reasons to celebrate, both big and small. Every celebration will make people that much more excited to continue the vision and try again with the next idea.

CONCLUSION

Erwin McManus wrote, "There is a critical distinction between managers who maintain organizations and leaders who create community by catalyzing movements. The former leader creates a corporation of people; the latter, a people with a cause."[11] I know God wants you to be one of those latter leaders. We have too many churches acting like organizations and managers rather than missional movements right now. We don't need any more in the church. What we need are people brave enough to be leaders and catalysts for the movement of God's Spirit.

Through these pages, we've covered a lot of concepts. Some of them I've been able to give you in great detail. About others, I've been intentionally vague because you have to do the hard work to apply the application to your situation. You need to examine where you are in your ministry, in your life, and in the life of your church so that you can, either individually or as a team, map out how to get to your goal. I hope that you've found a good map in these pages.

The Disney Corporation isn't the perfect company. They make mistakes like all companies do. I choose to focus on Disney in this book because Disney excels at bringing happiness to people. They are masters of creating an environment of quality service. They do so many things well that the church can, and should, emulate. Phil Card, Disney Cast Member and part of the InnerMission Theater touring group, told me that he felt being part of the Disney family complimented his faith because of Disney's core value of always exceeding guest expectations. Exceeding the expectations of others is something we should be driven to do out of love for God and neighbor, not merely as a way of doing good business. Disney provides a pattern that the church can see and emulate.

I don't want you, or your church, to try to be Disney. You can't. I don't care how large your church is, you'll never have the resources to do everything Disney does. But, even if you did, don't try. Don't try to be any other church, or leader, either. Be you. Be unique. Be who God created you to be.

We use emulation to help us learn. When I first started preaching, I tried to preach like several pastors I really respected. I modeled myself after what they did: I tried to talk like them, walk like them, and use their expressions. Often I would practice by preaching their sermons. As a young pastor, that was okay. Eventually, though, I found my own identity and now I preach like me. There are still elements of all of my role models existent in what I do, but I am more me than them. Or maybe I should say I am more the sum of all of them plus my unique take on life. Use the ideas in this book to get you started. Emulate the principles of what Disney has done, but don't try to copy them. Use their models and ideas to help you begin moving in the right direction. If you work through that process continually and faithfully, eventually you'll create a culture of excellence and creativity within your church or team that is unique to you. And that's when the magic truly begins.

My prayer is that the ideas in this book will be a true blessing to you and what you're trying to accomplish for God. I know God wants to bless you and others through you in ways that you can't begin to imagine. May the ideas of the Magic Kingdom lead you to accomplish great things for God's kingdom! If you can dream it, God can do it.

★

LIVING INTO THE LESSON

1. How are you allowing fear to stop you from implementing change? What are you willing to do to change this?

2. With whom do you want to share the information and vision you discovered in this book?

3. In thinking about the changes you want to make, what is first priority? What is important, but can wait?

4. What is your mission statement? How well are you fulfilling it? Is it adequate for the vision you have for your ministry or church?

5. How well is your vision statement fulfilling the mission of your ministry? Does it need to be updated? How?

6. Which Q1 issue will give you the quickest victory? How will you tackle it? How will it enhance your ministry?

7. What obstacles are you most likely to encounter in achieving your goals? How will you overcome them?

8. Chris speaks of "positive conflict." Do you (or your team) view conflict as positive or negative? What steps do you need to take to encourage more positive conflict?

9. What is your procedure for documenting your process? Is there anything you need to update to create complete documentation?

10. How will you encourage celebration of your victories?

11. What are you ready to do to accomplish God's reign here on earth?

★ NOTES ★

INTRODUCTION

1. *Aladdin*, DVD, directed by Ron Clements and John Musker (1992, Burbank, CA: Walt Disney Home Entertainment, 2004).

2. Philip Jenkins, *The Next Christendom* (New York: Oxford University Press, 2007).

3. Leonard Sweet, *Postmodern Pilgrims: First Century Passion for the 21st Century World* (Nashville: Broadman & Holman, 2000).

4. Hebrews 13:8.

5. *Beauty and the Beast*, DVD, directed by Gary Trousdale and Kirk Wise (1991, Burbank, CA: Walt Disney Home Entertainment, 2002).

6. I strongly recommend you go to www.disneyworld.com and check out the ads for further evidence of what I'm talking about. The Small World commercial can be seen at http://www.youtube.com/watch?v=aiOmeF1J1Hc.

7. Rita Mae Brown, *Sudden Death* (New York: Bantam Books, 1983), 68. It should be noted that this quote has also been variously attributed to Benjamin Franklin, Albert Einstein, Mark Twain, and an old Chinese proverb, but this is its first known appearance in print.

CHAPTER 1

1. *Hunt for Red October*, DVD, directed by John McTiernan (1990, Hollywood, CA: Paramount Pictures, 2003).

2. Bill Capodagli and Lynn Jackson, *The Disney Way: Harnessing the Management Secrets of Disney in Your Company* (New York: McGraw-Hill, 2007), 271–72.

3. Pat Williams, *How to Be Like Walt* (Deerfield Beach, FL: Health Communications, 2004), 232.

4. Brooks Barnes, "Is Disney's Chief Having a Cinderella Moment?" New York Times, April 9, 2010, business section, www.nytimes.com/2010/04/11/business/11iger.html?pagewanted=1, 2 (accessed October 21, 2010).

5. Ibid., 3.

6. Ibid., 4.

7. Chris Warner and Don Schmincke, *High Altitude Leadership* (San Francisco: Jossey-Bass, 2009), 36–37.

8. You can read it on the Disney corporate website: http://corporate.disney.go.com/careers/who.html.

9. Merriam-Webster Online Dictionary, s.v. "sanctuary," copyright 2010 by Merriam-Webster, Inc., http://www.merriam-webster.com/dictionary/sanctuary (accessed October 21, 2010).

10. Go to http://www.gbod.org and search for "safe sanctuaries" to learn more.

CHAPTER 2

1. Dave Smith, *Quotable Walt Disney* (New York: Disney Editions, 2001), 98.

2. Detlef Reis, "More Lessons from the Pixar Magician," *Thinkergy Journal*, Thursday, September 25, 2008, http://www.thinkergy.com/resources/articles/more-lessons-from-the-pixar-magician.html.

3. C. Wayne Perry, "First look: what brings clergy candidates into ministry and what happens when they don't get it," *The Journal for Pastoral Care* 57, no. 1 (2003).

4. Martin Luther, *Luther's Primary Works*, ed. Henry Wace and C. A. Bucheim (London: Hodder and Stoughton, 1896), 399.

5. John Calvin, *Institutes of the Christian Religion*, vol. 2, ed. John T. McNeill, trans. and index. Ford Lewis Battles (Philadelphia: Westminster Press, 1960), 1476.

6. Bill Capodagli and Lynn Jackson, *Innovate the Pixar Way* (New York: McGraw Hill, 2010), 68–72.

7. The Disney-Driven Life, "Neurotic Disney Person of the Month," http://thedisneydrivenlife.com/archives/4359, July 1, 2010.

8. These websites can be found at http://www.wdwautism.com, http://www.intercot.com, and http://allears.net/pl/special.htm.

9. Described on the Disney Parks Blog: http://disneyparks.disney .go.com/blog/2010/06/handheld-device-will-offer-detailed-descriptions -for-guests-with-disabilities-at-disney-parks/.

10. See http://disneyparks.disney.go.com/blog/2010/09/celebrating -international-deaf-awareness-week-at-disneyland-resort/.

11. An example is found at http://www.nicumc.org/pdf/adv/handicap accaudit.pdf.

12. See http://www.angelfoodministries.com.

13. The Dis Blog, "Marty Skyler Discusses Working with and for Walt Disney," posted December 18, 2009 by Dave Parfitt, http://www .disunplugged.com/2009/12/18/marty-sklar-discusses-working-with- and-for-walt-disney/ (accessed August 1, 2010).

14. See http://www.northpoint.org.

15. J. A. Jacobs. "Changing hours of employment in American families," paper presented at Workforce/Workplace Mismatch? Work, Family, Health, and Well-Being, Washington, D.C., June 16–18, 2003.

16. Elizabeth Vandewater, D. S. Bickham, and J. H. Lee, "Time well spent? Relating television use to children's free-time activities," *Pediatrics* 117/2 (February 2006):e181–91, available at pediatrics.aappublications .org/cgi/reprint/117/2/e181 (accessed August 11, 2010).

17. Wade Horn, "Time with Children Is Investment in Future," http://www.dadi.org/wh_time.htm (accessed August 11, 2010).

18. S. Hofferth and J. F. Sandberg, "How American children spend their time," *Journal of Marriage and Family* 63 (2001): 295–308.

19. See http://www.bigidea.com.

CHAPTER 3

1. Imagineers, *The Imagineering Way* (New York: Disney Editions, 2003), 20.

2. Dave Smith, *Walt Disney Famous Quotes* (Burbank, CA: Walt Disney Corporation, 1994).

3. Full transcription of his speech can be found at http://www.american rhetoric.com/speeches/mlkihaveadream.htm.

4. Bill Capodagli and Lynn Jackson, *Innovate the Pixar Way* (New York: McGraw Hill, 2010), 2.

5. Imagineers with Melody Malmberg, *Imagineering: A Behind the Scenes Look at Making More Magic Real* (New York: Disney Editions, 2010), 8.

6. Jeff Kurtti, *Since the World Began* (New York: Disney Editions, 1996).

7. Bill Capodagli and Lynn Jackson, *The Disney Way* (New York: McGraw Hill, 2007), 170.

8. Imagineers and Malmberg, *Imagineering*, 26.

9. Jason Garcia, "Disney says Fantasyland expansion plans are changing," *Orlando Sentinel*, The Daily Disney blog, August 12, 2010. http://thedailydisney.com/blog/2010/08/disney-parks-chief-fantasyland-expansion-plans-are-being-redrawn/ (accessed August 13, 2010).

10. ABC News, "Nightline: The Deep Dive," originally aired July 13, 1999.

11. Jack Blitch, NASA Information Technology Summit, delivered August 19, 2010, http://wdwmagic.com/Attractions/Ariels-Adventure/News/20Aug2010-CGI-video-walk-through-of-the-new-Little-Mermaid-attraction-being-built-in-Fantasyland.htm (accessed August 20, 2010).

12. Charles Arn, *How to Start a New Service* (Grand Rapids: Baker Books, 1997), 67.

13. Imagineers, *Imagineering Way*, 159.

14. Ibid., 206.

CHAPTER 4

1. Susan Veness, *The Hidden Magic of Walt Disney World* (Avon, MA: Adams Media, 2009), vii.

2. Nick Saban and Brian Curtis, *How Good Do You Want to Be?* (New York: Ballantine Books, 2007).

3. Andrew Carter, "Jimbo Fisher following the Nick Saban blueprint of program-building," *Orlando Sentinel*, January 18, 2010, http://blogs .orlandosentinel.com/sports_college_fsu/2010/01/jimbo-fisher-following -the-nick-saban-blueprint-of-program-building.html (accessed July 12, 2010).

4. There's a lot of research on the psychology of colors. Do a Google search and you can learn a lot in a short time.

5. Imagineers with Melody Malmberg, *Imagineering: A Behind the Scenes Look at Making More Magic Real* (New York: Disney Editions, 2010), 96.

6. You can contact UMCOR through http://www.umcor.org for information on the Connecting Neighbors program, which helps your congregation work out a detailed disaster response plan.

7. You can find plenty of great details about the Haunted Mansion at http://www.doombuggies.com and http://longforgottenhauntedmansion .blogspot.com. Some of these stories also came from interviewing Imagineers and Cast Members about the ride.

8. Christopher W. Perry, "Transmission and Reception of Blended Family Narratives in the Church Context," DMin diss., Asbury Theological Seminary, 2007.

9. Jim Collins, *Good to Great* (New York: HarperBusiness, 2001), 130.

10. Ibid., 47.

11. Bill Capodagli and Lynn Jackson, *The Disney Way* (New York: McGraw Hill, 2007), 202.

12. Ibid., 204.

13. Benjamin Zander and Rosamund Stone Zander, *The Art of Possibility* (New York: Penguin Books, 2002), 27.

14. You can read a lot more about servant evangelism at Steve Sjogren's website, http://www.servantevangelism.com/main.cfm. Steve was the pastor of Cincinnati Vineyard who started the servant evangelism movement.

CHAPTER 5

1. Carl Long, "Jitsu vs. Do," lecture delivered March 6, 2010, at Big Green Drum Dojo, Pensacola, FL.

2. J. Jeff Kober, *The Wonderful World of Customer Service at Disney* (Kissimmee: Performance Journeys, 2009), 16.

3. Lee Cockerell, *Creating Magic* (New York: Doubleday, 2008), 131.

4. Ibid., 115.

5. Tim Marshall, "Goshen United Methodist Church Damage Survey," March 1994, http://www.stormtrack.org/library/damage/goshen.htm (accessed May 19, 2010).

6. Rick Warren, *The Purpose Driven Church* (Grand Rapids: Zondervan, 1995).

7. Cockerell, *Creating Magic*, 132.

8. Johnny Lee, "Lookin' for Love (In All the Wrong Places)" on *Urban Cowboy: Original Motion Picture Soundtrack* (Los Angeles: Full Moon Records, 1980).

9. Jim Collins, *Good to Great* (New York: HarperBusiness, 2001), 41.

10. Ron Hunter Jr. and Michael E. Waddell, *Toy Box Leadership* (Nashville: Thomas Nelson, 2008), 138.

11. Jim Davis, Garfield comic strip, August 29, 2010, http://www.garfield.com/comics/todayscomic.html (accessed August 29, 2010).

12. Clinical pastoral education (CPE) is a structured program that takes place in a clinical environment such as a hospital, hospice, or prison, to teach future pastors how to more effectively minister to persons in a crisis situation. You can learn more at http://www.acpe.edu.

13. Steven Covey, *The Seven Habits of Highly Successful People* (New York: Simon and Schuster, 1989).

14. James L. Garlow, *The 21 Irrefutable Laws of Leadership* (Nashville: Thomas Nelson, 2002), 70–71.

15. Imagineers, *The Imagineering Way* (New York: Disney Editions, 2003), 63.

16. Ibid.

CHAPTER 6

1. Merriam-Webster Online Dictionary (http:/www.Merriam-Webster.com), © 2010 by Merriam-Webster, Inc.

2. Though this quote is widely attributed to Bishop Temple, I could not locate a detailed citation giving when or where he said it.

3. If you are not familiar with these movements, do a Google search and you'll find a good bit of information on the topics. Though I don't recommend it for serious research, Wikipedia also has good articles on both topics.

4. Robert Webber has written the most comprehensive thoughts on this emerging trend in worship. You can examine his ideas at http://www.ancientfutureworship.com.

5. Dan Kimball, *The Emerging Church* (Grand Rapids: Zondervan, 2003), 42.

6. Jeff Larson, "Lessons from Advertising," presentation at Creative Ministry Conference, Orlando, FL, Jan. 6, 2010.

7. Lee Cockerell, *Creating Magic* (New York: Doubleday, 2008), 208.

8. See http://www.willowcreek.com/summit.

9. See http://www.leadershipnexus.org.

10. See http://www.DisneyInstitute.com.

11. See the Leadership Institute link at www.cor.orgcatalyst/leadership/.

12. Larson, "Lessons from Advertising."

13. See http://www.census.gov.

14. Http://www.city-data.com and http://www.link2lead.com are two of the most common sites that help package the census data for you. Percept runs Link2Lead specifically for churches.

15. Jim Atchinson, "Creativity at SeaWorld," presentation at Creative Ministry Conference, Orlando, FL, January 8, 2010.

16. Joe Calloway, *Becoming a Category of One* (Hoboken: John Wiley & Sons, 2003), 53.

17. Ibid.

18. Richard Avery and Donald Marsh, "We Are the Church," © Hope Publishing, 1972.

CHAPTER 7

1. E. Stanley Jones, *Mahatma Ghandi: An Interpretation* (New York: Abingdon-Cokesbury Press, 1948), 51–52.

2. Nick Saban and Brian Curtis, *How Good Do You Want to Be?* (New York: Ballantine Books, 2007), 183–84.

3. Jim Collins, *Good to Great* (New York: HarperBusiness, 2001), 51.

4. Lee Cockerell, *Creating Magic* (New York: Doubleday, 2008), 253.

5. Found numerous places, such as: http://thoughts.forbes.com/thoughts /man-johann-wolfgang-von-goethe-treat-people-as.

6. *Meet the Parents*, directed by Jay Roach (CA: Universal Pictures, 2000).

7. Found at http://www.appleseeds.org/St-Fran_Preach-Gospel.htm (accessed August 1, 2010).

8. Rick Abbot, *Play On* (London: Samuel French, 1980), 73.

9. Erwin McManus, "The Barbarian Way," presentation at Willow Creek Leadership Summit, August 2003.

CHAPTER 8

1. Alice Bass, *The Creative Life* (Downer's Grove: Intervarsity Press, 2001), 40.

2. See http://www.brainyquote.com/quotes/authors/w/wayne_gretzky .html.

3. Bill Hybels, *Courageous Leadership* (Grand Rapids: Zondervan, 2002), 52.

4. If you're interested in a similar group for your church, you can find out more at http://www.spiritual-leadership.org/.

5. Check out the "Get Organized Community" link at http://www .franklinplanner.com.

6. Stephen Covey, *The 7 Habits of Highly Effective People* (New York: Fireside, 1989), 151.

7. A few examples: Andy Stanley, *Visoneering* (Sisters, OR: Multnnomah, 1999); Aubrey Malphurs, *Advanced Strategic Planning* (Grand Rapids: Baker Books, 2005); Bill Hybels, *Courageous Leadership* (Grand Rapids: Zondervan, 2009); and Mike Slaughter, *Unlearning Church* (Nashville: Abingdon, 2008). There are also several organizations that specialize in helping you develop your mission and vision statement such as Spiritual Leadership, Inc. and Leadership Nexus.

8. Http://www.goodreads.com/quotes/show/35678.

9. Http://www.youngentrepreneur.com/blog/uncategorized-blog/ quit-talking-begin-doing-walt-disney.

10. *Star Wars: Episode V: The Empire Strikes Back*, directed by George Lucas (San Francisco: Lucasfilm, 1980).

11. Erwin Raphael McManus, *An Unstoppable Force* (Loveland: Group, 2001), 134.

Other books from The Pilgrim Press

LEARNING TO TALK SHEEP
Understanding Those You Lead
Christopher W. Perry & C. Wayne Perry
978-0-8298-1850-5/paper/144 pages/$18.00

Based on more than ten years of research, *Learning to Talk Sheep* uses the common biblical image of the people of God as sheep and the pastor as their shepherd to describe the major types of personalities and members that every pastor will encounter. It offers guidance for pastors and lay leaders to work more efficiently and effectively with those they lead.

ENCOUNTERS AT THE COUNTER
What Congregations Can Learn About Hospitality from Business
Alan Johnson
978-0-8298-1817-8/paper/208 pages/$22.00

Encounters at the Counter shares Johnson's engaging face-to-face customer service. It explores the dimensions of retail hospitality that can be applied to congregations seeking to demonstrate genuine hospitality, such as the contagion of happiness, maximizing routines, renewing resources, taking time and making time, and promoting the quality of the product as well as the process.

I REFUSE TO LEAD A DYING CHURCH
Paul Nixon
978-0-8298-1759-1/paper/128 pages/$16.00

"God has called all leaders, lay and clergy, to lead healthy, growing spiritual movements. For this reason, I refuse to lead a dying church. And I invite you . . . to join me in refusing, ever again, to lead a dying church...." *—from the Introduction.*

To order these or any other books from The Pilgrim Press call or write to:

THE PILGRIM PRESS
700 PROSPECT AVENUE EAST
CLEVELAND, OHIO 44115-1100

Phone orders: 1-800-537-3394 • Fax orders: 216-736-2206
Please include shipping charges of $6.00 for the first book and $1.00 for each additional book.
Or order from our web sites at www.pilgrimpress.com and www.ucpress.com.

Prices subject to change without notice.